HARD
ASSETS

AND

HARD
MONEY

FOR

HARD
TIMES

HARD ASSETS
AND
HARD MONEY
FOR
HARD TIMES

A Blueprint to Build a Hard Asset Empire™
That Can Withstand Every Economic Cycle

Ben Reinberg

Published by:

I Own It Management, LLC dba Alliance Academy

1717 Deerfield Road, Suite 300S

Deerfield, IL 60015

Phone: +1 847-317-0077

www.benreinberg.com/book

www.alliancecgc.com/academy

Hardcover: 979-8-9924530-0-3 Softcover: 979-8-9924530-1-0

eBook: 979-8-9924530-2-7

Printed in the United States of America

First Edition 2025; Contributor & Editor: Chris J Snook; Foreword by Sharon Lechter; Cover Design: Thynkfuel Media

For permissions, inquiries, or bulk orders, please contact:

I Own It Management, LLC dba Alliance Academy

1717 Deerfield Road, Suite 300S

Deerfield, IL 60015

Phone: +1 847-317-0077

DEDICATION

To my incredible family, your unwavering love and support have been my foundation. To my dedicated team at Alliance Consolidated Group of Companies, your commitment and belief in our mission have made this journey possible. And to those who have shaped my career, mentored me, and challenged me to grow, this book is a testament to my lessons. It is to all of you that I dedicate this book.

~Ben Reinberg

TABLE OF CONTENTS

- The Fundamentals of Hard Assets
- The Fundamentals of Commercial Real Estate
- The Risk Return Spectrum
- War Stories:
    - Cash is King-The Battle to Stabilize My Portfolio in a Market Freefall
    - The Forgotten Scale: A Hard Lesson in Balancing Risk and Reward

---

ACKNOWLEDGEMENTS

Writing this book has been a journey of deep reflection, relentless dedication, and unwavering passion. It would not have been possible without the support, encouragement, and guidance of several remarkable individuals who have played a significant role in my life and work.

First and foremost, I extend my heartfelt gratitude to my family - my unwavering pillars of strength. Your support means the world to me.

To my colleagues, mentors, and friends who have challenged my thinking, broadened my perspectives, and contributed valuable insights along the way—thank you for inspiring me to push beyond limits and refine my vision. Your wisdom and encouragement have helped shape the essence of this book.

A special note of appreciation goes to my team @alliancecgc. In addition, our attorneys, brokers, marketing team, consultants, accountants, vendors, and every single resource that has helped me and my associates throughout these years, your dedication and commitment to excellence have been instrumental in shaping the ideas and principles that fill these pages. I am grateful for the opportunity to lead alongside such talented individuals.

To my readers—those who seek growth, wisdom, and excellence - this book is for you. I hope these words serve as a guide, a source of inspiration, and a reminder that wealth is not just about power or position but about purpose, impact, and legacy.

Finally, I give thanks to the lessons of experience, the challenges that forged resilience, and the moments of clarity that revealed new paths. Every step of this journey has been a privilege, and I am honored to share it with you.

With gratitude,

Ben

FOREWORD

There are certain moments when the right book finds you at exactly the right time. Ben Reinberg's *Hard Assets and Hard Money for Hard Times* is one of those books. In an era where economic uncertainty and technological disruption dominate the headlines, this book offers a steadying force—a clear blueprint for building wealth, preserving financial security, and creating a legacy that lasts. As someone who has dedicated my career to financial education and empowerment, I can confidently say that Ben has crafted a guide for investors and anyone seeking to build a financial fortress that withstands the tests of time.

My journey in financial literacy began decades ago, fueled by a desire to help others understand the principles of wealth creation and preservation. Whether it was co-authoring *Rich Dad Poor Dad* or mentoring business leaders, I've seen firsthand how the combination of education and action can transform lives. Ben Reinberg embodies this philosophy. He not only shares his knowledge, but he lives it - building a real estate empire that is a testament to the strategies and values he outlines in this book.

Why This Book Matters

One of the most striking aspects of this book is its timeliness. History has shown us that hard times are inevitable. Economic cycles rise and fall, governments overspend, and industries are disrupted. Yet, as Ben so eloquently explains, there are constants in this ever-changing landscape: those who control hard assets dictate the future.

Throughout history, wealth has been built and preserved by those who own the resources that societies need. Whether it's land, gold, or - more recently - digital assets like Bitcoin, hard assets remain the cornerstone of economic power. This book acknowledges that reality and provides a practical, actionable framework for navigating a world where financial stability often feels out of reach for many.

Ben's message is especially relevant today as people grapple with rising inflation, volatile markets, and the rapid pace of technological innovation. Feeling overwhelmed or paralyzed in such uncertainty is easy, but you will reduce risk and create multiple income streams by what you discover in these pages. Hard times also create opportunities for those who are prepared and Ben's blueprint will ensure you are one of them.

A Blueprint for Your Very Own Hard Asset Empire™

What sets this book apart is its structure. Ben has laid out a comprehensive framework anchored in foundational principles and built upon cornerstones and keystones that unify the entire system. Each chapter takes you deeper into building what he calls a **"Hard Asset Empire™."** It's a concept that resonates deeply with me because it's not about chasing get-rich-quick schemes or speculative investments. It's about creating a legacy that can withstand the storms of economic uncertainty and provide security for future generations.

Ben starts with the foundational elements: *transactional focus, capital diversification, actionable intelligence, and market positioning*. These are not abstract theories but practical strategies that guide you in building a financial foundation to support your ambitions.

The cornerstones: data-driven decisions, developing a diverse portfolio, discipline, and durability provide the cornerstones of your structure. They reinforce the foundational elements and ensure that your empire isn't just built for today's opportunities and is resilient enough to endure tomorrow's challenges.

The keystones, which include flexible deal structures, synergistic partnerships, integrated asset management, and scalable growth strategies, act as the connective tissue that binds everything together. This metaphor of constructing a financial fortress is compelling and deeply practical. It's a reminder that wealth is not built haphazardly; it requires intentionality, planning, and adaptability.

Why Ben Reinberg?

As an investor and thought leader, Ben Reinberg brings an unparalleled depth of experience to this book. He has invested through multiple economic cycles, from the Gulf War recession of the early 1990s to the Great Recession of 2008 and the COVID-19 downturn. Each challenge taught him invaluable lessons, which he shares openly and generously in this book.

But what truly sets Ben apart is his ability to combine practical expertise with a profound sense of purpose. This book isn't just about making money; it's about helping people create a foundation of security and opportunity for their families. Ben understands that wealth is not just a measure of financial success - it's a tool for empowerment, freedom, and lasting impact.

Ben's emphasis on actionable intelligence particularly inspires me. In today's world, information is everywhere, but actionable intelligence is rare. The strategies and tools he recommends, from data-driven decision-making platforms to cash flow management systems, are game-changers for anyone serious about building wealth.

Empowerment Through Education

One of the reasons I was so honored to write this foreword is that Ben's mission aligns so closely with my own. For decades, I've worked to empower people through financial education, whether it's teaching them how to get out of debt, build businesses, or invest in their future. *Hard Assets and Hard Money for Hard Times* continues that legacy by providing readers with the knowledge and tools they need to take control of their financial destinies.

This book also acknowledges a hard truth that is often overlooked: generational wealth is hard to build, easy to advance, and even easier to lose. Across cultures and centuries, the adage remains the same—wealth rarely survives beyond three generations. Ben's framework is designed to change that. By focusing on hard assets, disciplined management, and strategic planning, he provides a blueprint for creating a legacy that endures.

A Call to Action

As you turn these pages, I encourage you to approach this book as a manual and a mentor. Let Ben's experience guide, challenge, and inspire you to take action. Whether you're just starting your investment journey or looking to scale your existing portfolio, the principles and strategies in this book will meet you where you are and help you get to where you want to be.

The world is changing faster than ever, and our challenges can feel daunting. But as Ben so powerfully demonstrates, hard times are also opportunities for those who are prepared. By following the framework laid out in this book, you're not just building wealth—you're building a fortress, a legacy, and a future that you and your family can be proud of.

I am proud to call Ben Reinberg a peer and a friend, and I'm confident that this book will be a transformational resource for everyone who reads it.

Sharon Lechter
Author, Exit Rich, *Rich Dad Poor Dad* Co-Author, *Think and Grow Rich for Women* Entrepreneur, Mentor, and Financial Literacy Advocate

WHAT READERS HAVE TO SAY...

"A must-read for anyone serious about building and maintaining generational wealth." –Ryan Miller, BSc MFin, Global CEO at Pentium Capital Partners

"Ben Reinberg shares battle-tested investment wisdom and provides a usable blueprint that works in any market dynamic." –Jeff Hoffman, Founder of Priceline.com, Chairman of Global Entrepreneurship Network, Grammy and Emmy Award winner, Bestselling Author, Humanitarian

"This book is packed with real-world strategies, recommendations, resources, and personal war stories, not just theory." – Dan Fleyshman, Founder Elevator Studio

"The Hard Asset Empire Blueprint™ is the investment framework I've been searching for and will be a movement in personal finance the way Lean Startup took over how business plans and successful investment grade startups were built. This is a must read for every investor" – Chris J Snook, Managing Partner ATOMIQ Capital, Bestselling Author of *Digital Sense, Wealth Matters 3.0, & The Generative Organization*

"Ben Reinberg turns complex investing into actionable steps anyone can follow." – Amilya Antonetti, Bestselling Author of *Designing Genius*, World-renowned Behaviorist and Conflict Resolution Expert.

"If you want to build lasting wealth, this book is your guide." – Larry Namer, Founder of E! Entertainment, Author of *OffScript*

"Every investor should have this book on their shelf and revisit their Hard Asset Empire Blueprint™ annually at a minimum." – Greg Reid, Founder of SecretKnock™, 28-Time Bestselling Author, Filmmaker, Speaker, Entrepreneur

"Ben Reinberg's wisdom will save you from costly investment mistakes; He's the real deal." – Brandon Turner, Author of The Book on Rental Property Investing

"No fluff, no hype—just straight-up strategies and easy to follow frameworks and recommendations that work." – Hunter Thompson, Founder of Asym Capital

"This book is packed with real-world strategies, recommendations, resources, and personal war stories, not just theory." – Joseph Shalaby, Founder & CEO of E Mortgage Capital, Inc.

Introduction:

The Timeless Challenge of Generational Wealth

Change is the only constant in life. This truth is as undeniable today as it has been throughout humanity's recorded history. Economies rise and fall, technologies disrupt, and societal norms shift. Still, one enduring pattern remains: those who control society's hard assets dictate the collective future and secure their family's place at the table for future generations.

The challenge of building, sustaining, and preserving generational wealth is not a modern phenomenon. It has been a reflection, caution, and ambition topic across cultures.

- The Chinese proverb warns, "富不过三代" (*Wealth does not pass three generations*).
- An Arabic saying illustrates a similar trajectory: "*My grandfather rode a camel, my father drove a Mercedes, I drive a Land Rover, but my son will ride a camel.*"
- In English, the familiar adage says, "*The first generation builds it, the second maintains it, the third loses it.*"

Across continents and centuries, the message is the same: creating and maintaining wealth that spans generations is incredibly hard work. Advancing it is easier, but preserving it requires discipline, foresight, and adaptability. You are

25

reading this book at a pivotal moment in history. You know the stakes are high, whether you are building your first portfolio, recovering from a setback, or trying to grow and protect a legacy for future generations. You are keenly aware that as you read this book, we are witnessing the largest transfer of wealth in the history of humanity and don't want to be on the wrong side of that reality. Prices are rising, governments seem to be spending without restraint, and technological disruption alters industries faster than most can keep up. You're here because you need a blueprint that doesn't promise shortcuts or easy riches but offers a proven approach to building, advancing, and preserving wealth through hard assets and disciplined strategies.

This book is about ensuring that your *hard work* (ambition, effort, and vision) translates into *Hard Assets and Hard Money* - not just financial security for you and your family during *Hard Times* but also to seize the opportunities that will allow you and your future generations to thrive in the face of the challenges that lie ahead.

Why Did I Write This Book

This book isn't just another list of regurgitated principles of building wealth, as there are millions of those - it's personal for me and designed to be personally applicable and useful to you as you design a blueprint for your family's financial fortress and fulfillment. In short, this book is written to inspire you and provide a framework to customize your plan for generational wealth and for future generations to revisit it as needed to refresh it for modern times without ruining its solid foundation.

Like you, I want to continue to evolve and grow and make my next thirty years better than my last thirty. Therefore, this book is not designed to be the gospel of wealth but a digestible snapshot of my thinking and experience as I enter my 31st year of investing full-time and look ahead to what motivates and concerns me today so that you can hopefully enjoy more success with a lower-cost/impact of the necessary setbacks along the way.

My journey into commercial real estate began in the *hard times* of the early 1990s, a time when the Gulf War recession cast a shadow over the economy. The Federal Funds rate peaked at 8.25%, GDP shrank, and unemployment climbed to nearly 7%. Starting my career during such uncertainty shaped my approach to investing. I learned early on that *resilience and willpower aren't just buzzwords* - they are a necessary DNA strand to cultivate.

Over the past three decades, I've invested through multiple recessions, each with its challenges and lessons. The Gulf

War recession (1990-1991) taught me the importance of patience and the power of a long-term view. The Dot-Com Recession in 2001 reinforced the need for diversification as speculative markets collapsed while hard assets like real estate held steady. The Great Recession of 2007-2009 tested everything I had built. With GDP plummeting 4.3% and unemployment peaking at 9.5%, many investors panicked and sold at the bottom. However, I leaned into alternative financing, restructured my portfolio, and emerged stronger.

Most recently, the COVID-19 Recession in 2020 was a stark reminder of how quickly the rules can change. As the Fed Funds rate dropped nearly to zero and unemployment skyrocketed to 14.7%, cash flow became king, and adaptability was the difference between surviving and thriving. These economic downturns have reinforced the principles guiding this book: adaptability, disciplined cash flow management, diversification, and a deep understanding of market cycles.

2023 was so overpriced in our transactional focus area that we didn't acquire a single new property into the portfolio for one of the first times in my thirty years. Whereas 2024 was filled with several new opportunistic acquisitions and the firm's expansion into a couple of new asset classes in our forward-looking transactional focus, and we invested in the infrastructure of Alliance Consolidated Group of Companies in preparation for the massive opportunity table, we see being set up by the hard times and wealth transfer ahead.

These experiences shaped my investment philosophy and the framework I share in this book. Whether you're just beginning your journey or navigating the complexities of a growing portfolio, I aim to equip you with a blueprint for building wealth that endures across generations.

Like many of you, I started with a mixture of ambition and uncertainty, seeking stability in a world that seemed anything but stable. My early investments were riddled with mistakes, from underestimating property management complexities to overleveraging debt. Each misstep taught me invaluable lessons that shaped the framework in these pages.

One of the most defining moments of my career came during the 2008 financial crisis. I had spent years carefully building a portfolio, only to watch the stability I had worked so hard to create teeter on the brink as banks tightened their belts and markets panicked. Many investors folded during that time, but I refused to give in to fear. Instead, I adapted. By partnering with private lenders, restructuring financing, and acquiring distressed properties at a fraction of their value, I weathered the storm and emerged stronger. This experience reinforced a fundamental truth: adaptability and access to alternative capital are critical to long-term success.

I wrote this book to empower you with the lessons I've learned, the mistakes I've made, and the strategies that have proven resilient through decades of change. Whether you're a seasoned investor or just starting, I aim to provide you with the tools to build a strong financial foundation, seize opportunities during hard times, and secure a legacy for future generations.

A Blueprint To Withstand the Hard Times

Building a *Hard Asset Empire™* isn't a matter of chance—it's a matter of deliberate strategy and execution. Generational wealth is constructed brick by brick, guided by a clear vision, actionable intelligence, and unrelenting discipline. At the core of this endeavor lies a framework supported by four essential cornerstones: *Data* (actionable intelligence), *Development* (portfolio construction), *Discipline* (cash flow management), and *Durability* (resilience planning).

These cornerstones form the foundation of a blueprint designed to help you build wealth that not only withstands economic uncertainty but thrives during it. Let's explore these principles deeply and understand how they work together to create a financial fortress.

Data: Actionable Intelligence

In the age of information, data is power—*but only if* it is actionable. The most successful investors don't simply gather information; they harness it from human, artificial, internal, and external feeds to analyze and apply it to make timely and well-informed decisions. Actionable intelligence is the data cornerstone that allows you to identify trends, discern the impact of external forces, uncover opportunities, and avoid pitfalls before they materialize.

For instance, understanding demographic shifts, like the aging population's impact on healthcare demand, can guide investments in medical office buildings. Similarly, tracking macroeconomic trends, such as interest rate movements or inflation patterns, can inform decisions on financing structures and asset allocation.

Modern tools and technologies give investors a significant edge, from AI-driven analytics platforms to specialized real estate market reports. At Alliance, we have begun executing a multi-year plan that embraces the digital transformation of our company, fund, and industry operations. We have started initiatives around our proprietary *Alliance Acquisition Engine™* that will dramatically duplicate my thirty years of deal experience by 100-1000 fold in the coming years and also launched our Alliance Intelligence™ division and newsletter as we build new capacity on top of this cornerstone in our own business to drive more efficiency to our day-to-day operations and decision making.

Data doesn't replace intuition or experience but amplifies your effectiveness when refined into actionable intelligence. By grounding your strategy in actionable intelligence, you ensure that every decision is supported by evidence, reducing risk and maximizing potential returns.

Development: Portfolio Construction

Diversification is the cornerstone of any resilient portfolio, and how you develop your portfolio is critical to its ability to weather any economic storm. You reduce risk and create multiple income streams by spreading investments across multiple property types, geographic regions, hard asset classes, and financial structures. This strategy ensures that no single market or economic downturn can threaten the integrity of your portfolio.

Consider the diverse roles of different asset classes:

- Multifamily properties offer stability during housing shortages and economic downturns.
- Medical office buildings thrive across market cycles due to the consistent demand for healthcare services.
- Industrial warehouses benefit from the continued growth of e-commerce and logistics.
- Gold and Bitcoin provide stores of value and liquidity for idle cash reserves, protecting against inflation and currency devaluation.
- Dividend-paying stocks and businesses offer both cash flow and potential capital appreciation.

Diversification isn't just about risk mitigation—it's a strategy for capitalizing on opportunities. By positioning your portfolio across complementary asset classes, you ensure that while one sector may face challenges, others will continue to perform. This approach creates a portfolio that survives economic shifts and also grows stronger as a result.

Discipline: Cash Flow Management

Cash flow is the lifeblood of any investment empire. Managing it effectively isn't simply about balancing the books—it's about planning for the unexpected and ensuring liquidity to seize opportunities when others are constrained.

Every investment should be evaluated for its cash flow potential. It's easy to be seduced by high appreciation projections, but if an asset doesn't generate sufficient income to cover expenses, it can quickly become a liability. Operating expenses, from maintenance costs to vendor contracts, must be scrutinized and controlled to protect profit margins.

Discipline also means maintaining reserves. Economic downturns are inevitable, and having sufficient liquidity allows you to weather periods of uncertainty without selling assets at unfavorable terms. During these times, cash flow discipline becomes a strategic advantage. While others are forced to retrench, disciplined investors can act decisively, acquiring distressed assets or securing favorable terms on new deals.

Durability: Resilience Planning

Resilience is the ability to withstand and recover from setbacks; durability ensures that your investments are built to endure. Economic downturns, regulatory shifts, and unexpected challenges are not hypothetical—they are guaranteed. Planning for these events before they occur is the difference between surviving and thriving.

Resilience planning begins with stress-testing your portfolio. Consider worst-case scenarios: How would a significant interest rate hike impact your cash flow? What happens if occupancy rates drop unexpectedly? Running these scenarios allows you to identify vulnerabilities and address them proactively.

Flexible financing is another critical component. Fixed-rate loans and long-term debt structures can provide stability while maintaining liquidity reserves ensures that you can pivot when opportunities or challenges arise. Finally, having multiple exit strategies for each investment ensures that you're never backed into a corner. Whether through refinancing, asset sales, or buyouts, having options gives you control even in turbulent times.

Resilience is also about mindset. Those who panic during economic downturns often miss the opportunities that come with them. A well-prepared investor, by contrast, can act boldly, acquiring undervalued assets or renegotiating favorable terms. Durability ensures that you're not just surviving hard times but capitalizing on them.

Building Wealth to Endure

When combined, these four cornerstones—*data, development, discipline, and durability*—lay on top of the foundation of a blueprint designed to build wealth that withstands the hardest of times. Each cornerstone supports the others: actionable intelligence informs investment strategies, cash flow discipline reinforces resilience, and diversification ensures that your data-driven insights are applied across a balanced portfolio.

Building a **Hard Asset Empire™** isn't about chasing trends or taking unnecessary risks. It's about constructing a financial fortress designed to endure. Generational wealth is not built overnight, but with a clear plan and unwavering commitment to these principles, you'll create a legacy that stands the test of time.

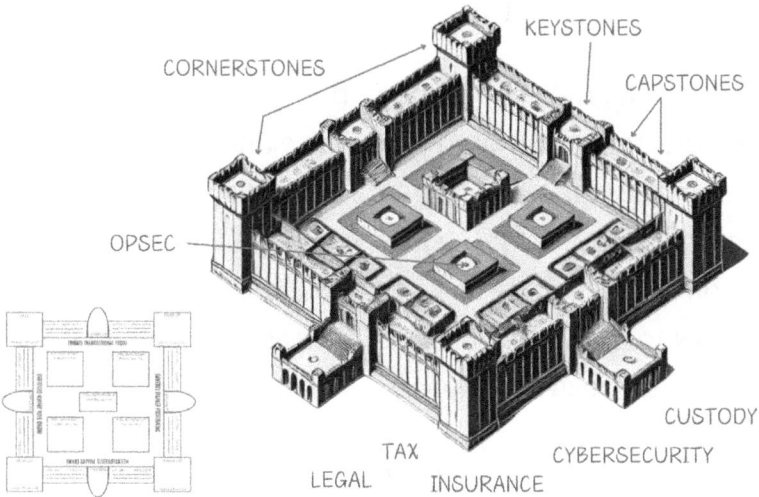

HARD ASSET EMPIRE BLUEPRINT™

KEYSTONES

CORNERSTONES

CAPSTONES

OPSEC

CUSTODY

TAX CYBERSECURITY

LEGAL INSURANCE

The storms will come, as they always do. But with this blueprint, you can face them confidently, knowing that your financial foundation is strong, your portfolio is diverse, and your strategy is durable. This is not just about surviving the hard times—it's about thriving through them and emerging stronger on the other side.

The Generational Hard Asset Empire Blueprint™

As you embark on this journey, remember that the goal isn't just to build wealth—it's to build wealth that endures.

Generational wealth requires a blueprint considering the foundation and the other core elements of time-tested design. It also requires a vision for how to accumulate hard assets and protect and secure them over time.

This book will guide you through the principles, strategies, and lessons forged through experience and history. From understanding the timeless value of hard assets to navigating modern disruptions confidently, you'll gain a comprehensive playbook for success. When you reach the final chapter, you'll know how to build your financial fortress and ensure it stands strong for future generations.

Throughout this book and through my e-courses on www.alliancecgc.com/academy you will be able to download and also interact with my AI-powered brain to fill in and personalize your own **Hard Asset Empire Blueprint™**.

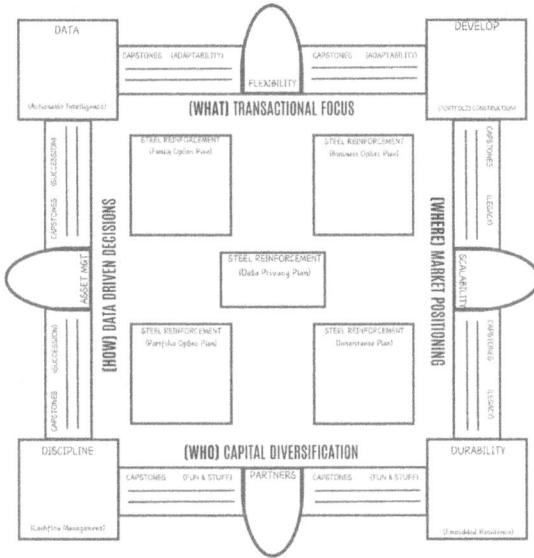

MY HARD ASSET EMPIRE BLUEPRINT ™

FAMILY NAME:

Summary

Generational wealth is hard to build, easy to advance, and even easier to lose. As history shows, the stakes are high. But with the right blueprint, you can rise to meet this challenge, creating not just financial stability but a legacy that endures. Let's get started.

Endnotes

1. Robert T. Kiyosaki and Sharon Lechter, *Rich Dad Poor Dad: What the Rich Teach Their Kids About Money That the Poor and Middle Class Do Not!* (Warner Books, 1997), 142.
2. Thomas J. Anderson, *The Value of Debt in Building Wealth* (Wiley, 2016), 56–58.
3. Richard H. Thaler, *Misbehaving: The Making of Behavioral Economics* (W.W. Norton & Company, 2015), 124–128.
4. United States Bureau of Labor Statistics, "Consumer Price Index Summary," https://www.bls.gov/.
5. John P. Kotter, *Leading Change* (Harvard Business Review Press, 1996), 75–80.

SECTION ONE:

CORE FOUNDATIONS

1

Understanding Hard Assets

The world seems to be moving faster than ever, with rising prices and technological disruption leaving many feeling like they're working harder just to stay afloat. Watching those with hard assets grow exponentially wealthier while struggling to maintain a current lifestyle can be demoralizing. It's not just inflation eating away at paychecks—it's the sense that the rules of the game have changed, and those without a blueprint are being left behind.

This book offers a sober yet invigorating solution. It's not a get-rich-quick scheme but a proven plan to build a resilient financial foundation that grows and protects your wealth over time. Hard assets—tangible, intrinsic-value investments like commercial real estate, gold, land, and even Bitcoin—are the cornerstone of this strategy. They offer a way to keep up and thrive amid economic uncertainty and technological change.

In this chapter, we'll explore the concept of hard assets, their role in financial stability, and why they've become indispensable today. We'll then dive deeper into commercial real estate, a standout subset of hard assets, and understand its potential to generate cash flow and long-term wealth.

The Fundamentals of Hard Assets

Hard assets are more than investments—they are shields against uncertainty and building blocks for generational wealth. Unlike paper investments such as stocks or bonds, which are vulnerable to market speculation and economic policy shifts, hard assets derive value from their intrinsic or productive qualities.

What Are Hard Assets?

Hard assets encompass a wide variety of tangible and intrinsic-value investments. Each offers unique benefits, and together they form the foundation of a diversified wealth-building strategy:

- **Precious Metals**: Gold, silver, and platinum have stood the test of time as stores of value, particularly during periods of inflation or currency instability.

- **Land** is famous for being the oldest form of wealth preservation. It remains finite but often appreciates over time.
- **Commercial Real Estate (CRE)**: Income-generating properties such as multifamily apartments, office buildings, and industrial warehouses combine tangible value with consistent cash flow.
- **Bitcoin and Cryptocurrencies**: Bitcoin has emerged as "digital gold," or, as Michael Saylor believes, "Crude Capital," offering a decentralized hedge against inflation and monetary debasement and a potentially unparalleled source of permanent collateral.
- **Cash-Flow Generating Assets**: Rental properties, dividend-paying businesses and equities, or similar. In that case, all investments provide steady income streams.

Hard Assets Matter Now More Than Ever

The appeal of hard assets lies in their ability to hedge against inflation, economic downturns, and geopolitical uncertainty. Given today's ballooning government debt and disruptive technological change, holding assets with intrinsic value is essential. Consider gold's historic role as a refuge during financial crises or Bitcoin's rise as a store of value in the digital age. Similarly, cash-flowing assets like commercial real estate preserve wealth and actively grow it through consistent income.

The Fundamentals of Commercial Real Estate

Commercial real estate stands out as a wealth-building powerhouse among all hard assets. It offers the dual benefits of tangible value and income generation, making it a keystone for those looking to build long-term financial stability.

Commercial Real Estate Is Still My First Love

Unlike hard assets that rely on price appreciation to generate returns, commercial real estate offers cash flow through tenant leases while benefiting from long-term appreciation. When you factor in the tax benefits of depreciation expenses, this is like a triple threat that still gets my juices flowing every time I look at a deal. Not to mention there is something very satisfying about driving by something and saying to myself, "I own it!".

This triple combination of cash flow, long-term appreciation, and tax benefits makes it both a defensive and offensive strategy in your financial arsenal and a very tangible and emotionally satisfying one as you level up as a Hard Asset Empire™

Economic Drivers of Commercial Real Estate

CRE is shaped by a variety of economic forces: agnostically

- **Population Growth**: A growing population increases demand for multifamily housing and urban infrastructure.
- **Urbanization**: The shift toward cities drives demand for office spaces, retail locations, and industrial facilities.
- **Technological Advances**: The rise of e-commerce has transformed industrial real estate, with warehouses and logistics centers now among the hottest sectors.

Understanding these drivers helps investors predict demand and identify lucrative opportunities.

The Role of Leverage

Leverage is a defining feature of CRE, allowing investors to amplify their purchasing power. By using debt strategically, investors can acquire larger properties with smaller amounts of equity, thereby increasing potential returns. However, leverage must be managed carefully to avoid excessive risk, especially during economic downturns.

The Different Types of Commercial Real Estate

Commercial real estate is not a monolith. It encompasses a range of asset types, each with unique characteristics and opportunities:

1. **Multifamily Properties**: Consistently in demand, multifamily housing offers stable cash flow and is often considered a safe haven during economic uncertainty.
2. **Office Buildings**: These properties vary widely in risk and return, with suburban business parks offering stability and urban high-rises presenting growth potential in the right markets.
3. **Retail Spaces**: While traditional retail has faced headwinds from e-commerce, experiential-use and mixed-use developments remain strong performers.
4. **Industrial Properties**: Warehouses and logistics centers have seen explosive demand driven by e-commerce and supply chain innovations.

5. **Specialty Properties**: From healthcare facilities to student housing, these niche investments offer high returns for those with specific expertise.

The Risk-Return Spectrum

Commercial real estate offers opportunities across a wide risk-return spectrum. Understanding where an asset falls on this spectrum is essential for aligning investments with your goals and risk tolerance:

- **Core Properties**: Low-risk assets in prime locations that generate stable income.
- **Core-Plus**: Moderate-risk properties with minor improvement potential.
- **Value-Add**: Medium- to high-risk investments requiring significant renovations or operational upgrades.
- **Opportunistic**: High-risk projects involving redevelopment or major repositioning.

Successful investors often balance their portfolios with a mix of these categories, diversifying across asset types, locations, and risk profiles to mitigate volatility and enhance returns.

Two Personal War Stories from the Alliance Vault

The Day I Almost Lost It All – How Building an Emergency Fund Saved My Empire

In the early 2000s, I was a young and hungry investor, building my portfolio brick by brick, deal by deal. Real estate was my passion, craft, and ticket to generational wealth. I had already notched a few solid wins, and like any ambitious entrepreneur, I pushed forward aggressively.

Then came the deal that almost wiped me out.

The Perfect Storm: A Bad Market, a Bad Partner, and a Bad Break

It was an office campus in St. Louis—a massive 300,000-square-foot property spanning two floors. At its peak, it was home to a high-profile Berkshire Hathaway tenant, providing steady rental income and a strong valuation. The deal looked bulletproof. But, as I would learn the hard way, nothing is truly bulletproof in commercial real estate.

The market took a nosedive, and a major tenant bailed. Suddenly, what had been a stable, income-producing asset became a sinking ship.

To make matters worse, the loan came due, and the bank—facing its crisis—wasn't interested in working with us. We were over-leveraged, and the tightening credit markets meant refinancing was off the table.

I was the majority partner, but I was tangled up with a partner who wasn't pulling his weight. He refused to step up when things got tough, leaving me to navigate the chaos alone.

And then came the real nightmare: We had to sell the property—but not to just any buyer. It went to a shark, someone who knew our position and used it to their advantage.

The worst part? I had personally guaranteed the loan, and the original bank wouldn't sell us the loan or refinance me during the workout period despite my being able to buy the note out at a discount. Instead, they sold the note to a third-party private equity firm in New York that became the new lender. Their leverage was that they wanted the property, and I was in the way.

This wasn't just a deal gone bad—it was now personal, and I was in the deep end with professional confiscators who would use every trick in the book to take advantage of a young man new to the business.

Fighting for Survival

For two long years, I fought to stay afloat and to hold on to the asset, not lose my young career, and felt like David against Goliath. Ultimately, my advisors told me that the most important thing was not to keep the property but to get the personal guarantee removed. What that ultimately meant was going to the new note holders and offering to give them the property if they removed my personal guarantee and let my guys structure the deal from a tax standpoint in a certain way to take a huge loss and give them control at the new basis. This ultimately was how we did the workout plan, and the net operating loss carried forward ended up helping me take huge tax-free gains on multiple deals in the following years.

- *The lender was ruthless, using my personal guarantee as a weapon against me.*
- *The IRS code gave me a way out (more detail on page 235). Using one of its provisions, I purposely took a huge tax hit from canceling debt on this deal to remove my personal guarantee and structure the takeover terms to help me in the future.*
- *The market was in crisis mode, drowning in a full-blown recession. Hence, macro forces and smart advisors gave me the air cover to survive any reputational risk perceived by existing or future investors. I showed that I knew how*

to not die on the battlefield during a loss but to live another day and ensure that my future victories would be tax-advantaged.

- *I barely slept. The anxiety was overwhelming, but ultimately I learned how the game is played at a different level, and the experience was priceless.*
- *I faced the terrifying reality that if this went sideways, I could lose everything, but only if I let that be how the story and my career ended.*

The Turning Point

This wasn't just a financial battle—it was a test of my resilience.

One thing saved me: I had an emergency fund.

It wasn't massive, but enough to cover essential business expenses. Enough to fight another day. Sufficient to ensure that, no matter what, I wouldn't be wiped out completely.

And then, in the middle of this storm, I met someone who would change my career forever: Dave Wabick.

Dave had been in the trenches before. He had seen market cycles come and go, and he gave me one critical piece of advice:

"Ben, you're not the only one who's been here. This will pass. You just have to stay in the game."

That conversation stuck with me and earned me my stripes with a new level of peers in the market who no longer saw me as just an ambitious kid but as a battle-tested investor who could get his teeth kicked in but get back up and keep fighting and finding value in the market.

I doubled down on my relationships, staying in touch with investors even when I didn't have good news. I communicated more frequently because silence breeds fear, and I needed my stakeholders to know I wasn't hiding. This was how I clawed my way back.

Lessons Learned: The Hard Truths of Commercial Real Estate

I came out of that deal scarred but smarter. And I never made those same mistakes again.

Here are the hard truths I took away:

1. The personal guarantee trap: Never sign a personal guarantee unless you fully understand the consequences. The lender will use it against you when things go wrong.
2. The partner problem: Partnerships are only as strong as the weakest link. Choose your business partners as carefully as you choose your investments.

3. *Communication is everything. Investors care about more than returns—they care about transparency. Silence is deadly in a crisis and breeds distrust and fear. Keep people informed, even when the news isn't good.*
4. *Overleveraging is a killer. Debt is a great tool when used wisely, but too much leverage with no margin for error is a ticking time bomb.*
5. *Emergency Funds Aren't Optional: Having liquid capital is the difference between surviving and getting wiped out. Keep reserves—because the market doesn't care about your plans.*

The Diamond in the Rough

Losing that deal was painful. But it was also a turning point in my career. It forced me to become a better investor, a better leader, and a better steward of capital, and in the process, I introduced someone who would become a trusted colleague for life.

This business will test you. It will take you to the edge. But if you build the right habits, surround yourself with the right people, and always keep cash reserves, you can take the punches and keep moving forward.

The Most Important Lesson: The Ability to Hold

That experience properly reinforced another key principle: **The ability to hold** *a hard asset and carry it through rough times, so you can sell it when the market is ripe. Likewise, if you can acquire one from someone who can't hold on during the hard times like the New York private equity guys did from me, then you can benefit from the massive gains when the market cycles back up again.*

I learned this lesson again during my first syndication deal—the Holste Property in Northbrook, IL (60089). It was an industrial property, an odd L-shaped building, which made it hard to lease.

The first week after I took over, we lost a tenant. The remaining tenants were heavily concentrated in steel manufacturing, making more than 45% of the building's occupancy tied to one industry—a risky setup.

But I held.

Because I knew that if I could **carry the property long enough,** *I could sell it when the market was in my favor. And when that time came, the deal paid off.*

The ability to hold is everything.

Building your Hard Asset Empire™ will occasionally push you to the edge. But if you develop the right habits, surround yourself with the right people, and **always keep cash and relationship reserves**, you can take the punches and keep moving forward.

I almost lost everything early on, but instead, I learned how to build an empire that could withstand anything. This book contains the blueprint-building framework I developed to help you organize and implement your strategy to weather any economic storm.

Cash is King-How Liquidity Saved the Deal

Some deals test your strategy. Some deals test your patience. And then there are the ones that test your sheer will to fight. The **Stater Bros. Deal** in Fountain Valley, Orange County, was one of those deals. It was complex, ruthless, and nearly disastrous—but it taught me one of the most important lessons in real estate: **Cash is King.**

The Sandwich Lease Gamble

Unlike my other deals, where I typically acquired hard assets outright, this one was a **sandwich lease**. In this rare and complicated structure, you lease a property from one owner and then sublease it to another party. In this case, I held a **leasehold interest**, meaning I didn't own the property—just the lease agreement. I planned to raise $1M and structure a profitable re-lease with **Stater Bros., a strong grocery store chain and the anchor of the deal.**

On paper, it looked like a winner. Every store was golden—an essential, high-traffic tenant that guaranteed stability. But in real estate, nothing is guaranteed.

The Pay-or-Quit Nightmare

I was confident in the deal, but I hadn't accounted for **a landlord with a decades-old agreement with a hidden landmine buried deep in the language: a pay-or-quit clause.** If a tenant failed to pay rent for any reason, even a disputed invoice, the landlord had the right to evict them immediately.

That clause sat dormant for years until suddenly, **I received a ridiculous invoice**. The charge was so outrageous that it was clearly a setup. But the moment that invoice landed, it triggered the pay-or-quit rule.

I was facing an impossible situation—either pay an absurd and unjustified charge or risk losing the entire deal.

The Legal Fight for Survival

The only way to protect my position was to hire one of the best real estate litigators in the country, **an expert in pay-or-quit** *clauses.* *It wasn't an option—it was a necessity. But expertise like that doesn't come cheap. Legal fees quickly climbed north of $1 million.*

Without steady cash flow, I wouldn't have stood a chance. If I didn't have liquid capital ready, I would have been another victim of predatory legal tactics. They would have squeezed me out, walked away with my leasehold, and left me with nothing.

The case dragged on for a year and a half. The fight was ruthless. The landlord and their legal team were greedy, relentless, and willing to do anything to force me out. The battle culminated in a deep money trial, where I sat in a courtroom, defending my position against a state trust with a bad lawyer. It was a knock-out, drag-down fight that tested every ounce of my resilience.

The Result: A Hard-Earned Victory

*After **18 months of legal warfare**, the judge ruled in my favor. The landlord's bad faith tactics were exposed, and their case unraveled. But even though I won, the deal **had drained an enormous amount of time and resources**—far more than I had ever expected for what started as a relatively small deal.*

Lessons Learned: The Price of Doing Business

1. **Be Careful Who You Surround Yourself With.** Bad partners and unethical landlords can cost you dearly. Choose your business relationships wisely.
2. **Time is Your Most Valuable Asset.** Some deals simply aren't worth the time they consume. This one soaked up much time and energy that could have been better spent elsewhere.
3. **Read Every Word.** Details matter in life, and a **forgotten word in contracts can haunt you forever.** The hidden pay-or-quit clause almost cost me everything.
4. **Cash is King.** Without liquidity, you can't fight. This deal proved to me that strong cashflow isn't just about profit but survival. **When things go wrong, cash is your greatest weapon.**
5. **I Can Get Through Anything.** This deal was a war, but it also reinforced something deep in me—**no matter how hard a deal gets, I'll find a way to win.**

Some deals make you money. Others make you stronger. This one did both—but it came at a steep cost. And it's one I'll never forget.

Summary

Hard assets are paramount to a resilient financial fortress strategy, unique for their ability to protect and grow wealth during uncertain times. By examining the fundamentals of hard assets and diving deeper into commercial real estate specifically, we've set the stage for understanding why this category is paramount to generational wealth-building.

Hard assets like CRE combine tangible value, cash flow, and long-term appreciation, offering a proven path for those ready to break free from the hamster wheel of trying to keep up. With the fundamentals and types of CRE explored the next chapter will delve into the framework you can use to build your **Hard Asset Empire™**. The next step is diving deeper into the blueprint and tools that help make your vision a reality.

Endnotes

1. Andrew Bailey, *Hard Assets: The Ultimate Wealth Protection* (Cambridge Publishing, 2021), 45–50.
2. Saifedean Ammous, *The Bitcoin Standard*, 2018), 150–153.
3. Robert Kiyosaki with Sharon Lechter, *Rich Dad's Guide to Investing* (Plata Publishing, 2012), 92–95.
4. Deloitte, "2023 Real Estate Outlook," https://www.deloitte.com/.
5. Urban Land Institute, *Emerging Trends in Real Estate 2024* (ULI, 2024), 40–45.

2

Building Your Hard Asset Empire™

Every great empire, whether physical or financial, is built on a solid foundation. In the world of real estate and hard money investing, this foundation is your framework—the bedrock beneath a financial fortress capable of withstanding any attack or storm, whether predicted or unforeseen. Without it, even the most ambitious plans will crumble under pressure. With it, you gain the resilience and adaptability needed to thrive through economic cycles and capitalize on opportunities others might overlook.

Building this fortress isn't about luck or guesswork, and building generational wealth isn't just about accumulating assets—it's about constructing a fortress capable of withstanding the tests of time. Those controlling hard assets throughout history dictated the future, secured their families' legacy, and influenced the economic landscape. Yet, the challenge of creating and preserving generational wealth remains daunting. Chinese proverbs warn that wealth rarely survives three generations. Across cultures, this universal truth endures: wealth is hard to build, easy to advance, and even easier to lose.

A clear, deliberate framework is essential today, marked by economic uncertainty and technological disruption. This chapter presents the blueprint for building a hard asset empire whose foundation is rooted in four essential design elements:

The Hard Asset Empire™ Foundational Elements:

1) WHAT: (Transactional Focus),

2) WHO: (Capital Diversification),

3) WHERE: (Market Positioning), and

4) HOW: (Data-driven Decisions)

These are not just abstract concepts—they are foundational process ingredients that the cornerstone and keystone actionable strategies are built upon, that will guide your investment decisions, stabilize your portfolio, and set you on a path to long-term success.

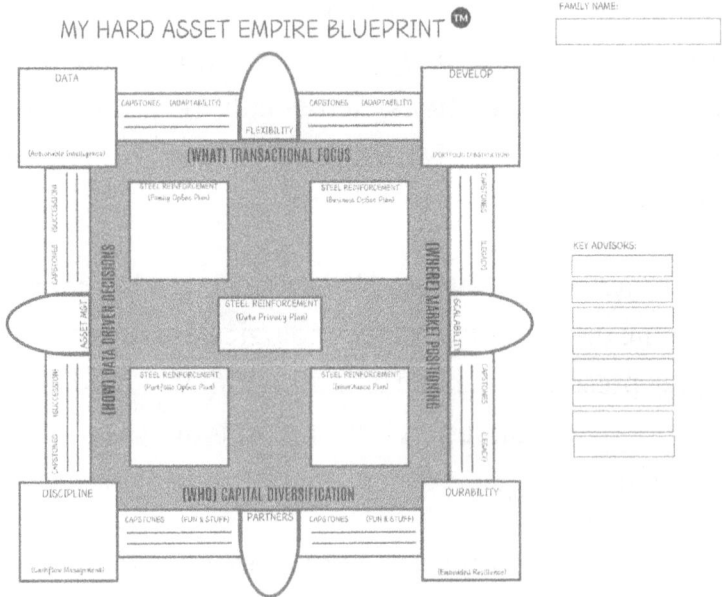

Essential Elements of a Firm Foundation

WHAT: Transactional Focus - Defining Your Core Strengths

The first step in laying your foundation is deciding where to focus your efforts. Not all transactions are created equal, and *the deals you pursue will shape the trajectory of your investment journey.* Your transactional focus should align with your expertise, resources, and long-term vision.

For some, this means allocating capital to firms that are targeting large, complex projects like high-rise developments or luxury mixed-use properties. Take JVP Management as an example. Their specialization in sophisticated transactions, such as the $1.2 billion refinancing of Extell's Upper West Side condo tower, illustrates how a focused strategy can build a reputation, attract institutional capital, unlock more significant opportunities, provide personal enjoyment, and integrated operation at the Alliance Consolidated Group of Companies provides investors the benefits of a diversified portfolio of assets with a historical 28% IRR (Internal Rate of Return), that has been de-risked by our integrated operation that makes it easier to enter multiple geographies within a select group of asset classes where decades of deep relationships unlock rare opportunities for your money to be to ensure value-added projects or multifamily acquisitions may be more appropriate for others, particularly those just starting. These deals require less capital, pose fewer risks, and provide a manageable learning curve. Successfully executing a value-added project builds confidence and teaches critical skills in operations, financing, and tenant management. Over time, these smaller victories create a foundation of experience that propel you to more ambitious transactions.

Transactional focus isn't just about what deals you take on; it's about understanding your core strengths and leveraging them to achieve your goals. This focus keeps your foundation grounded, helping you filter out distractions and align every decision with your broader strategy.

WHO: Capital Diversification - Building Financial Stability

A fortress's foundation needs strong reinforcement to support its structure, and in the financial world, the rebar in your foundation comes from having diverse capital sources. Capital source diversification is essential for creating a resilient and flexible investment strategy that can withstand market volatility and economic storms.

Consider JVP Management's approach to capital diversification. With $3 billion in assets under management and over $2 billion from institutional investors like insurance companies, they have built a funding base to pursue high-value projects confidently. This diversified structure ensures they are not overly reliant on a single source of capital, which can be risky in fluctuating markets.

An individual investor's journey to capital diversification often begins with private lenders, traditional bank loans, or partnerships with family and friends. As your portfolio grows, tapping into institutional capital—such as family offices, private equity funds, or pension plans—becomes a natural next step. The broader your funding base, the less vulnerable you are to changes in interest rates, lending policies, or macroeconomic conditions. Remember that in every market, capital is moving, and the key is to make sure that when it stops moving your way from one source, you have another source to draw upon to take advantage of your next opportunity.

Capital diversification isn't just about accessing more money; it's about creating financial stability and flexibility. By cultivating relationships with various funding partners and exploring innovative financing structures, you ensure your empire has the resources to grow and adapt. When someone asks you where you will get the money, you can jokingly say "wherever it is right now", but it's important to ensure that your foundation is filled with plenty of diverse reinforcements for capital access.

WHERE: Market Positioning - Choosing Your Battlefield

A fortress must be strategically placed to defend against threats and capitalize on opportunities. Similarly, market positioning involves understanding where to operate and what sectors to target.

For new investors, the journey often begins in familiar markets, whether that's a hometown or a sector they know well. These "home court" advantages allow you to navigate local regulations, build relationships, and leverage unique insights. When I got started, I focused on building my reputation as a principal and commercial real estate expert in my hometown market in Chicago, Illinois. Over the decades, I built upon that and dominated other markets in my transactional focus, which now has us successfully acquiring and operating properties across the country.

As your portfolio and experience grow, expanding into new geographies or sectors becomes a way to scale and diversify.

Cale Street, the investment arm of the Kuwaiti Sovereign Wealth Fund, provides an excellent example of thoughtful market positioning. By targeting U.S. commercial real estate debt deals, they strategically focus on stable, high-value markets with strong growth potential. Their approach ensures that their investments remain defensible and profitable, even in volatile times.

Staying ahead of macroeconomic trends is another key aspect of market positioning. The rise of e-commerce, for instance, has driven demand for industrial warehouses. At the same time, demographic shifts, remote working trends, and other post-Covid migration trends have created sustained opportunities in multifamily housing. By aligning your investments with these trends, you position your portfolio to thrive in the present and adapt to the future.

Market positioning isn't just about finding the right opportunities—it's about claiming your space within them. With a clear understanding of your battlefield, you can build a strong portfolio, regardless of economic conditions.

HOW: Data-Driven Decisions - Turning Insights into Action

In today's fast-paced investment landscape, actionable intelligence is more critical than ever. Data-driven decision-making isn't just a buzzword or concept—it's a cultivated habit and honed business process that provides the competitive advantage that separates the best investors from the rest. Collecting, analyzing, and acting on reliable data enables you to identify opportunities, mitigate risks, and position your portfolio for long-term success.

For example, demographic data can reveal high-growth areas where housing or industrial space demand will likely increase. Climate resilience and geospatial data from sources like www.alphageo.ai allow more sophisticated investors to look for geographic arbitrage opportunities within their portfolio. Economic indicators, such as interest rate trends or inflation forecasts, can guide financing strategies and asset allocation. Investors can make informed decisions that align with market realities by staying ahead of macroeconomic trends.

Modern tools, like AI-driven analytics platforms and market research reports, amplify the effectiveness of data-driven strategies. Subscribing to resources such as the **Alliance Intelligence Newsletter** at https://subscribetoben.com provides critical insights, ensuring you remain informed and prepared to capitalize on emerging trends. Scan the QR code to get my weekly intelligence and insights now.

Data doesn't replace experience or intuition—it enhances them. When integrated into your decision-making process, data becomes the glue that holds your foundation together, ensuring every move you make is grounded in evidence and aligned with your strategy.

Building a Resilient Foundation

The What, Who, Where, and How (Transaction focus, capital diversification, market positioning and data-driven decisions), form the foundation of a resilient financial empire. Together, these elements provide the clarity, stability, and adaptability needed to navigate the complexities of real estate and hard money investing.

But a foundation isn't static—it evolves. Markets shift, opportunities arise, and challenges emerge. Continuously refining and strengthening these cornerstones ensures that your financial fortress remains strong and prepared for whatever comes next.

With this foundation in place, you're not just building investments—you're on your way to building a legacy. Now, as we move through the rest of the framework, let's begin to define the cornerstones on top of this foundation.

3

The Cornerstones:

Stabilize Your Hard Asset Empire™

Building a hard asset empire is no different from constructing a physical fortress. Just as a fortress requires a solid foundation to withstand external pressures, your Hard Asset Empire™ financial fortress needs stabilizing cornerstones to weather economic cycles and capitalize on opportunities. Resting on top of your empire's foundation, your fortress is supported by four D's as the essential cornerstones: **Data (actionable intelligence), Development (portfolio construction), Discipline (cash flow management), and Durability (resilience planning).**

These cornerstones form the foundation of a blueprint designed to help you build wealth that not only withstands economic uncertainty but thrives during it. Let's explore these principles deeply and understand how they work together to create a financial fortress.

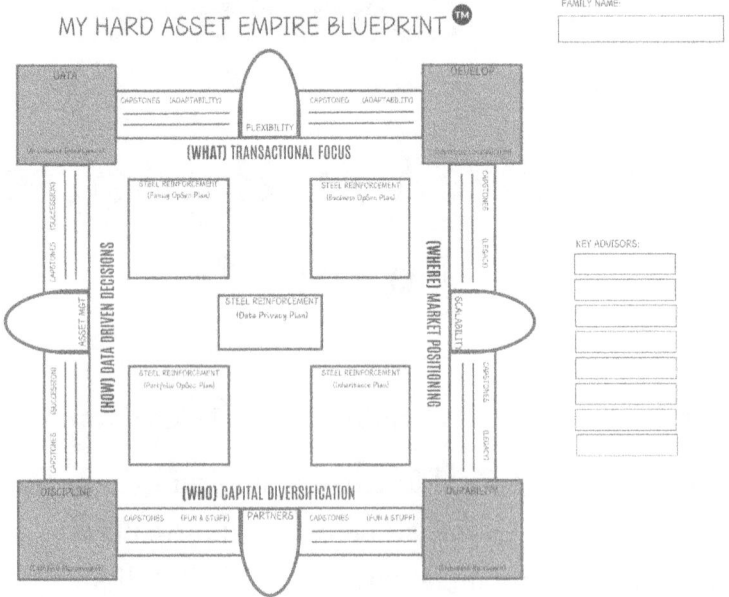

MY HARD ASSET EMPIRE BLUEPRINT™

Cornerstone One: Data-Actionable Intelligence

In the competitive world of commercial real estate and hard asset investing, success hinges on more than instinct or luck—it demands a cornerstone of actionable intelligence and insights. While foundational strategies provide stability, actionable intelligence elevates decision-making, enabling you to precisely seize opportunities and mitigate risks.

Raw data alone isn't enough; refining, analyzing, and applying that data transforms it into a competitive advantage. In today's digital landscape, data exhaust—the massive amounts of information generated by daily activities—is abundant. The challenge lies in converting this overwhelming resource into actionable insights.

For those serious about building a **Hard Asset Empire™**, creating an actionable intelligence system isn't just helpful—it's essential. Here's how to construct one step by step and recommend tools to consider as you begin implementing this cornerstone.

MY HARD ASSET EMPIRE BLUEPRINT ™

DATA

DEVELOP

CAPSTONES (ADAPTABILITY)   CAPSTONES (ADAPTABILITY)

FLEXIBILITY

[WHAT] TRANSACTIONAL FOCUS

STEEL REINFORCEMENT (Timing Option Plan)   STEEL REINFORCEMENT (Resource Option Plan)

STEEL REINFORCEMENT (Data Privacy Plan)

STEEL REINFORCEMENT (Portfolio Option Plan)   STEEL REINFORCEMENT (Governance Plan)

[HOW] DATA DRIVEN DECISIONS

ASSET MGT

[WHERE] MARKET POSITIONING

SCALABILITY

KEY ADVISORS:

DISCIPLINE   [WHO] CAPITAL DIVERSIFICATION   DURABILITY

CAPSTONES (RUN & STUFF)   PARTNERS   CAPSTONES (RUN & STUFF)

(Cash flow Management)   (Embedded Resilience)

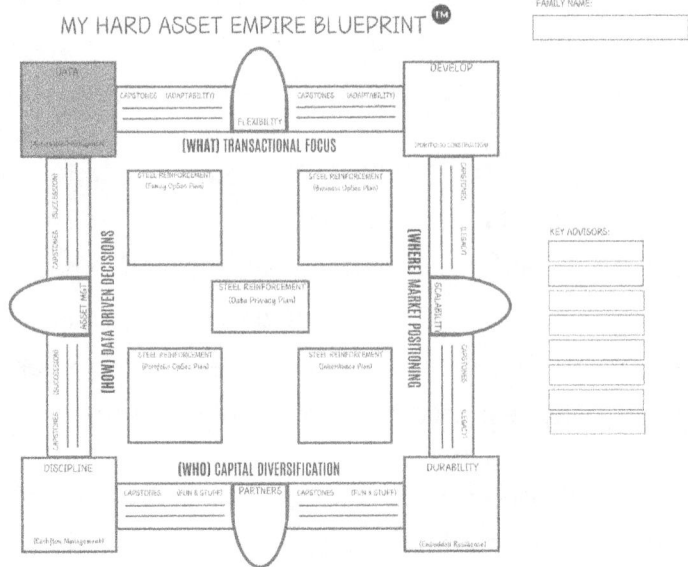

1. Defining Objectives and Metrics

The first step in creating an actionable intelligence system is to define your investment objectives and identify the metrics that matter most. Whether focused on multifamily housing, value-add office spaces, or industrial properties, your system should align with your investment goals and strategies.

Key Metrics to Consider:

- **Cap Rates**: Evaluate a property's return potential.

- **Vacancy Rates and Absorption**: Understand market supply and demand dynamics.
- **Market Trends**: Identify growth areas and sector performance.
- **Comparable Sales**: Assess property valuation and pricing benchmarks.
- **Economic Indicators**: Inform timing and market positioning.

Tool Recommendation: Begin with **Yardi Matrix** for deep market insights, **Crexi** or **CoStar** for a comprehensive view of real estate trends. These platforms offer robust data sets tailored to commercial real estate investors.

By clearly defining your metrics, you ensure that your system focuses on the information most critical to your decision-making process, eliminating the noise and honing in on actionable intelligence.

2. Collecting and Integrating Data

Effective actionable intelligence requires collecting high-quality data from multiple sources and integrating it into a centralized platform. This integration ensures consistency and efficiency, enabling data access and analysis from a single hub.

Data Sources to Explore:

- **Market Data Providers**: Platforms like **CBRE Market Insights** and **Reonomy** for comprehensive property and transaction data.
- **Demographic Tools**: Use **Esri ArcGIS** or U.S. Census Bureau data to track population growth, employment trends, and income levels.
- **Economic Indicators**: Federal Reserve Economic Data (FRED) or **Moody's Analytics** provide insights into interest rates, inflation, and broader economic shifts.

Tool Recommendation: Consider implementing a real estate-focused **Customer Relationship Management (CRM)** platform like **DealPath.** This platform allows you to aggregate data sources and track deal flow in one place. At Alliance, we have integrated **Hubspot (CRM)** for another option in case you run multiple businesses and want something broader.

Centralizing your data ensures it's not only accessible but also easily comparable across deals and markets, saving time and reducing errors.

3. Refining Data with Automation and AI

Once data is collected, the next step is refinement—turning raw information into actionable insights. Automation and AI tools streamline this process, enabling you to analyze large data sets efficiently and with fewer errors.

Technologies to Consider:

- **Automated Valuation Models (AVMs):** Tools like **Zillow Analytics** or **Skyline AI** use machine learning to provide instant property value estimates and assess risk.
- **Predictive Analytics:** Platforms like **Prophia** analyze lease and market data to forecast trends, tenant behavior, and the intended use of property performance.
- **Work flows:** Use tools like **Zapier** or **Monday.com** to automate repetitive tasks such as lead tracking, deal management, or financial modeling.

Tool Recommendation: Start with **Skyline AI** or **Alpha Geo** for predictive analytics. It's AI-driven insights can help you identify undervalued assets or future high-growth markets.

Automation and AI allow you to extract patterns and insights from large data sets, enabling you to prioritize opportunities and address risks before they materialize.

Note to the reader. Getting started with a tool like the above is a great way to start fast and get something in place to make better decisions. When you are growing into your first few million or billion in assets under management (AUM) I encourage you to re-invest in your own customized enterprise level AI agent platform to own your data and replace unnecessary SaaS (software-as-a-service) third party software with your custom AI brain stack like we have recently with our Alliance REI Nexus platform, but when you are building your empire you quickly realize there will always be new ground to conquer. We go deeper into some of these techniques in our courseware and live workshop on the Alliance Academy, so visit https://alliancecgc.com/academy and dive in when you wanna put this into action.

4. Visualizing Data with Dashboards

Visualization is the bridge between insight and action. A well-designed dashboard or report can distill complex trends into clear, actionable insights. Tools for data visualization turn raw numbers into charts, graphs, and reports that are easy to understand.

Applications for Visualization:

- **Market Opportunity Dashboards**: Highlight high-growth areas based on demographic and economic data.
- **Portfolio Performance Reports**: Track cash flow, expenses, and occupancy rates across your holdings.
- **Deal Comparisons**: Visualize side-by-side comparisons of properties based on metrics like ROI and risk profile.

Tool Recommendation: Start with **Tableau** or **Power BI**, which integrate seamlessly with many CRMs and data sources. They allow you to customize dashboards to your specific needs.

Clear visualization tools ensure that your actionable intelligence is not buried in spreadsheets but readily available to inform quick, confident decisions.

5. Building Feedback Loops

Actionable intelligence isn't static—it evolves. Building feedback loops into your system ensures it remains relevant and effective as your portfolio and markets change.

Key Feedback Mechanisms:

- **Post-Investment Analysis**: Regularly evaluate the performance of completed deals to validate or refine your criteria.
- **Collaborative Reviews**: Share dashboards and insights with your team to uncover blind spots or areas for improvement.
- **Iterative Updates**: Update your data sources, tools, and KPIs based on new trends, technologies, or business goals.

Tool Recommendation: Consider using **Slack** or **Asana** for team collaboration and sharing insights in real-time. Integrating these with your CRM ensures seamless communication across your operation.

Feedback loops turn your system into a dynamic tool that grows more sophisticated over time, ensuring it adapts to changing needs.

6. Actionable Insights: From Intelligence to Execution

The ultimate goal of actionable intelligence is to drive decisions that create value. Whether identifying undervalued properties, optimizing financing terms, or timing a sale, every insight should lead to action.

Example Applications:

- Use demographic trends to target secondary markets with high growth potential.
- Leverage economic data to secure financing before interest rate hikes.
- Evaluate deal flow dashboards to prioritize high-ROI opportunities.

Tool Recommendation: Pair **RealPage** for property analytics with **DealPath** for tracking and executing your acquisition pipeline.

Actionable intelligence empowers you to make faster, more informed decisions, turning insights into competitive advantages.

Cornerstone One Summary:

Constructing an actionable intelligence system is critical for navigating the complexities of hard asset investments. By integrating the right tools—like **CoStar**, **Tableau**, or **Crexi**—and continuously refining your processes, you can transform overwhelming data into a strategic weapon

The ability to extract actionable insights from data doesn't just help you compete—it positions you to lead. Start building your system today and ensure your Hard Asset Empire™ is fueled by clarity, confidence, and precision.

Cornerstone Two: Development - Portfolio Construction

Diversification is more than a buzzword in investment—it's the reinforcement mechanism that fortifies your portfolio against economic turbulence. It ensures that no single market downturn or asset class underperformance can jeopardize your financial stability. In the **Hard Asset Empire Blueprint™**, diversification plays a central role in creating a robust, adaptable portfolio capable of withstanding challenges while capitalizing on opportunities.

Portfolio diversification is a step-by-step process that combines deliberate asset selection, geographic strategy, and financial structuring. Let's explore how to develop a diversified portfolio using actionable strategies, tools, and practical examples.

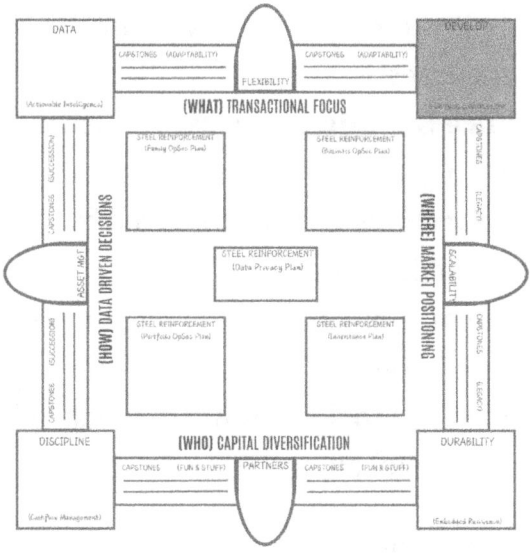

MY HARD ASSET EMPIRE BLUEPRINT ™

FAMILY NAME:

(WHAT) TRANSACTIONAL FOCUS

(HOW) DATA DRIVEN DECISIONS

(WHERE) MARKET POSITIONING

(WHO) CAPITAL DIVERSIFICATION

KEY ADVISORS:

The Principles of Diversification

Diversification involves spreading investments across multiple property types, geographic regions, hard asset classes, and financial structures. This strategy minimizes the risk of overexposure to a single market, while creating complementary income streams.

Consider the advantages of blending these asset classes:

- **Multifamily Properties**: Stability during housing shortages and recessions.
- **Medical Office Buildings**: Consistent demand driven by healthcare needs.
- **Industrial Warehouses**: Growth fueled by e-commerce and logistics.
- **Gold and Bitcoin**: Inflation-resistant stores of value for idle cash reserves.
- **Dividend-Paying Stocks and Businesses**: Reliable cash flow and capital appreciation.

By diversifying into complementary sectors, you ensure that your portfolio doesn't just weather market shifts—it thrives through them.

Step 1: Identify Your Investment Goals

Before constructing a portfolio, define your long-term objectives just like you would approach any other multi-faceted development project. *Are you focused on cash flow, capital appreciation, or wealth preservation, and in what weighting or priority?* Your goals will influence the asset mix and allocation within your portfolio.

For example:

- If **cash flow** is your primary goal, prioritize multifamily properties, dividend-paying stocks, or triple-net lease (NNN) assets like Medical Office Buildings (MOB).
- If **capital appreciation** is the aim, focus on value-add opportunities in emerging markets or industrial properties with high growth potential.
- If **wealth preservation** is key, allocate excess cash reserve sitting on the sidelines in money market funds to gold, Bitcoin, and Class A commercial properties in prime locations, especially when blood is in the streets from repricings or sharp changes in the bond market.

Tool Recommendation: Use financial planning software like **WealthTrace** or **Personal Capital** to simulate portfolio performance scenarios and align allocations with your objectives.

Step 2: Allocate Across Asset Classes

Diversification begins with allocating capital across complementary hard asset classes. This step ensures that different segments of your portfolio perform independently of each other, reducing overall risk.

Examples of Asset Class Diversification:

- **Multifamily Properties**: These assets provide stability and steady cash flow, even during economic downturns. Rent payments create reliable income streams, while long-term appreciation builds equity.
- **Medical Office Buildings**: Healthcare facilities offer recession-resistant opportunities due to the consistent demand for medical services.
- **Industrial Warehouses**: The surge in e-commerce and global logistics has driven demand for industrial spaces, making them a high-growth asset class.
- **Gold and Bitcoin**: Allocating 5–10% of your portfolio to these hard assets protects against inflation and currency devaluation, while maintaining liquidity for unexpected opportunities.
- **Dividend-Paying Stocks and Businesses**: These provide dual benefits of regular income and capital growth, complementing the stability of physical hard assets.

Tool Recommendation: Platforms like **Fundrise** and **CrowdStreet** provide access to diversified real estate investments across multiple asset classes, allowing you to start small and scale. If you are allocating larger amounts of capital and like the passive diversification of the platforms above but with a more personal white-glove approach, then I'd love to talk with you about being one of our limited partners at Alliance, and you can request a one-on-one call with our team or me at https://www.alliancecgc.com

Step 3: Geographic Diversification

Geographic diversification protects against regional economic downturns or localized risks, such as overbuilding in a specific market or regulatory changes. Expanding into different cities, states, or even countries ensures your portfolio remains resilient to localized volatility.

How to Approach Geographic Diversification:

- Begin with your local market, where you have the advantage of familiarity and established relationships.
- Expand into secondary markets that offer higher cap rates and growth potential, such as cities experiencing population growth or infrastructure investment.
- Gradually add investments in prime international markets, such as major European capitals or fast-growing Asian cities.

Tool Recommendation: Use tools like *Esri Business Analyst, CBRE Market Insights,* or *AlphaGeo.ai* to analyze population trends, job growth, climate resilience, geospatial data, and economic indicators in target regions.

Step 4: Financial Structuring for Resilience

Diversification extends beyond asset types and geographies—it also applies to how you finance your investments. A well-structured portfolio includes a mix of debt and equity, ensuring financial flexibility during growth and downturns.

Components of Financial Structuring:

- **Equity Investments**: Offer higher returns through appreciation and cash flow but require upfront capital. Equity positions are ideal for long-term wealth building.
- **Debt Investments**: Senior loans or mezzanine financing provide steady, predictable income with reduced risk exposure. These are perfect for stabilizing cash flow.
- **Creative Financing Options**: Consider leveraging joint ventures, partnerships, or syndications to diversify risk and access larger deals.

Tool Recommendation: *RealPage Investment Management* can help track financing structures and evaluate the impact of leverage on portfolio performance.

Step 5: Incorporate Alternative Assets

Alternative assets like gold, Bitcoin, or dividend-paying businesses add another layer of diversification, providing liquidity and inflation protection. These assets ensure that your portfolio remains agile and adaptable to macroeconomic shifts.

How to Allocate Alternative Assets:

- Allocate 5–10% of your portfolio to gold or Bitcoin, using platforms like **Vaulted** or **Swan Bitcoin** for secure storage and easy access. If you are allocating more than $500,000 at a time or multiple 7 or 8 figures to this asset, then you would want to look at a bespoke brokerage experience with someone like Secure Digital Markets (https://www.sdm.co) as you can do large Over-the-Counter (OTC) purchases, get bespoke lending products against your Bitcoin collateral up to 65% LTV with very competitive interest rates and an average 5-day closing period, as well as customized Covered-Call Option strategies for your Bitcoin.

- Invest in dividend-paying businesses or REITs through platforms like **M1 Finance**, which allow you to build custom portfolios with minimal fees.

Alternative assets serve as your portfolio's "insurance policy," providing stability and quick liquidity when needed for your excess cash reserves that you don't want just sitting in your money market account.

Step 6: Monitor and Adjust

Diversification is not a "set-it-and-forget-it" strategy. Regularly monitoring and adjusting your portfolio ensures it remains aligned with your objectives and responsive to changing market conditions.

How to Monitor and Adjust:

- Conduct quarterly performance reviews to evaluate cash flow, occupancy rates, and asset appreciation.
- Stay informed about macroeconomic trends impacting your holdings, such as interest rate changes or population shifts.
- Rebalance allocations annually to maintain your desired level of diversification.

Tool Recommendation: Use an enterprise AI agent platform to customize your portfolio management software, as we have with our **Alliance REI Nexus. This will allow you** to track asset performance, streamline reporting, maintenance alerts, lease expirations, and automate the scoring of potential acquisitions or dispositions.

Case Study: A Diversified Portfolio in Action

DISCLAIMER: *This is NOT FINANCIAL ADVICE. It is merely a simple theoretical example to illustrate the content above in a summary.*

Imagine an investor starting with a $1 million portfolio:

1. They allocate $500,000 to a Class B multifamily property in a secondary market, generating consistent cash flow.
2. They invest $200,000 in an industrial warehouse near a central logistics hub, benefiting from e-commerce growth.
3. They put $150,000 into a medical office building, ensuring stability through healthcare demand.
4. They hold $100,000 in Bitcoin and gold for liquidity and inflation protection.
5. The remaining $50,000 is invested in dividend-paying REITs for additional cash flow.

This diversified approach positions the investor to weather downturns in any single sector while capitalizing on growth opportunities across multiple asset classes.

Cornerstone Two Summary:

Development of a portfolio is built around diversification. Diversification is the backbone of a resilient portfolio and the second cornerstone of the **Hard Asset Empire Blueprint™**. By thoughtfully allocating across asset classes, geographies, and financial structures, you reduce risk and create multiple income streams that support long-term growth.

The process requires discipline and a commitment to regular monitoring, but the rewards are significant: a portfolio that not only withstands economic shifts but thrives because of them. Start small, leverage the recommended tools, and expand methodically. The result will be a diversified empire capable of enduring challenges and capturing opportunities for generations to come.

By following these principles and leveraging these tools, you can construct a portfolio that is as dynamic and adaptable as the markets it operates within. Now let's go to the third cornerstone.

Cornerstone Three: Discipline-Cash Flow Management

Cash flow is the lifeblood of any hard asset empire. Without disciplined management, even the most promising investments can become liabilities. The cornerstone of cash flow management is balancing income and expenses. It's about planning for the unexpected, maintaining liquidity, and ensuring your portfolio can thrive in uncertain times. In the **Hard Asset Empire Blueprint™**, cash flow discipline transforms financial uncertainty into opportunity, positioning you to grow when others are constrained.

This cornerstone addresses the critical components of cash flow management, providing actionable strategies and tools to ensure your investments consistently deliver value.

MY HARD ASSET EMPIRE BLUEPRINT™

FAMILY NAME

DATA

DEVELOP

FLEXIBILITY

(WHAT) TRANSACTIONAL FOCUS

KEY ADVISORS

(HOW) DATA DRIVEN DECISIONS

(WHERE) MARKET POSITIONING

(WHO) CAPITAL DIVERSIFICATION

PARTNERS

DURABILITY

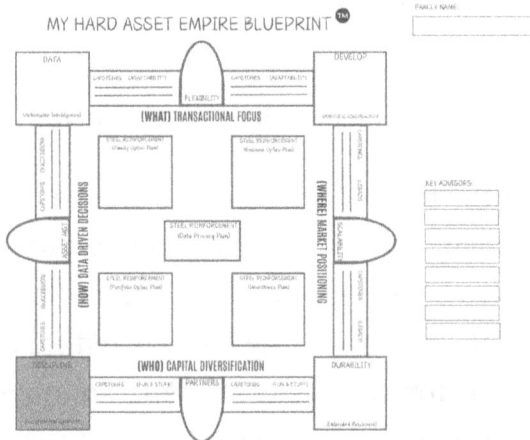

Understanding the Role of Cash Flow

Positive cash flow is more than a metric—it's a strategic advantage. A property that generates more income than it consumes in expenses ensures financial stability, allowing you to weather market downturns or capitalize on emerging opportunities. Conversely, properties with negative cash flow can quickly drain resources, creating vulnerabilities in your portfolio.

Effective cash flow management begins with assessing the income-generating potential of every deal. While high appreciation projections might look appealing, they cannot replace consistent, reliable income stability. An asset's cash flow determines its ability to cover operating expenses, service debt, and contribute to your overall financial health.

Tool Recommendation: Use **Stessa** or **Buildium** to track and optimize property-level cash flow. These platforms offer insights into income, expenses, and performance metrics, helping you make informed decisions.

Evaluating Investments for Cash Flow Potential

Before acquiring any asset, conduct a detailed cash flow analysis. This involves estimating potential rental income, calculating operating expenses, and projecting net operating income (NOI). Here's a step-by-step approach:

1. **Estimate Income**: Consider current rental rates, market demand, and tenant turnover. For commercial properties, include potential income from parking, signage, or ancillary services.
2. **Calculate Operating Expenses**: Include property taxes, insurance, maintenance, utilities, and management fees. Be conservative in your estimates to avoid surprises.
3. **Project Net Operating Income (NOI)**: Subtract operating expenses from gross rental income to determine the NOI. This figure is crucial for evaluating the property's profitability and debt coverage capacity.

4. **Stress-Test Assumptions**: Assess how changes in occupancy rates, rental income, or expenses might impact cash flow. Ensure the asset remains viable under less-than-ideal conditions.

Tool Recommendation: *Argus Enterprise* is an industry-standard software for detailed cash flow modeling and scenario analysis, particularly for commercial properties.

Controlling Operating Expenses

Maintaining healthy cash flow requires strict control of operating expenses. Overspending on maintenance, utilities, or vendor contracts can erode profitability, while inefficiencies in property management may lead to missed opportunities.

Strategies for Expense Management:

- **Negotiate Vendor Contracts**: To ensure competitive pricing, regularly review and renegotiate contracts for landscaping, cleaning, or maintenance.
- **Implement Preventative Maintenance**: Proactive maintenance reduces the risk of costly repairs and extends the lifespan of critical systems.

- **Monitor Energy Efficiency**: Upgrading HVAC systems or installing smart thermostats can lower utility costs and improve NOI.
- **Optimize Property Management**: Use professional property management firms with proven track records to streamline operations and reduce tenant turnover.

  Note to reader: An advanced strategy as you grow is to look at what we did at Alliance. Over the decades, we built our solutions for each piece of this vendor stack, from property management to a construction division and maintenance team, as part of our consolidated group of companies. This is an additional way to de-risk our cash flow outlays at the fund while tapping into additional income sources they represent at the parent company.

Tool Recommendation: Platforms like **Yardi Breeze** or **AppFolio** can help monitor and optimize operating expenses. They offer tools for budgeting, vendor management, and energy tracking.

The Importance of Liquidity and Reserves

Liquidity safeguards against the market's inevitable uncertainties. While cash flow keeps your portfolio operational, reserves provide the cushion to weather economic downturns, unexpected repairs, or tenant vacancies. Maintaining sufficient reserves ensures navigating these challenges without resorting to unfavorable asset sales.

Reserve Management Guidelines:

- **Set Reserve Targets**: Aim to maintain 3–6 months of operating expenses as a liquidity buffer for each property.
- **Allocate Emergency Funds**: Based on the property's age and condition, keep separate reserves (15-25% of NOI) for major repairs, such as roof replacements or HVAC upgrades.
- **Create Opportunity Funds**: Designate reserves for strategic acquisitions during market downturns, allowing you to purchase distressed assets or renegotiate deals.

Tool Recommendation: Use **Quicken for Real Estate** or **PropertyMatrix** to track and allocate reserves across your portfolio.

Seizing Opportunities with Cash Flow Discipline

Cash flow discipline is not just about survival—it's about positioning yourself to grow when others are forced to retreat. During economic downturns, many investors become constrained by limited liquidity or negative cash flow. Disciplined investors, however, can act decisively, acquiring undervalued assets or negotiating favorable financing terms.

For example, during the 2008 financial crisis, properties with strong cash flow and disciplined management were better able to withstand the downturn. Investors with sufficient reserves could purchase distressed assets at significant discounts, setting the stage for substantial growth during the subsequent recovery.

In 2024, as I am writing this book, history is repeating with over $2,000,000,000,000 ($2Trillion) of commercial mortgage paper will mature in the coming 18-20 months, and some estimates are as high as $2.5T. This means that at an average Debt Service Coverage Ratio of 1.25, roughly $3-$3.5T worth of commercial real estate assets will be repriced since the interest rates available today are more than double when the debt originated. Since CRE is valued off of its cash flow and more than $3T worth of asset values are about to be grossly underwater as the long-term leases or vacancy rates don't support a refinance at present rates, a MAJOR and unparalleled buying opportunity on pristine assets long term is coming to those with cash on hand in the coming months and years.

Strategies for Opportunistic Investing:

- **Monitor Distressed Assets**: Use platforms like **Crexi** or **Reonomy** to identify properties in financial distress.
- **Leverage Cash Flow Surpluses**: Allocate excess cash flow to fund acquisitions or secure lines of credit for future investments.
- **Engage Flexible Financing**: Establish relationships with lenders offering bridge loans or hard money financing to act quickly on time-sensitive opportunities.

Tool Recommendation: Platforms like **RealPage Portfolio Analytics** can help identify underperforming assets in your portfolio and optimize cash flow to fund new opportunities.

Feedback Loops for Continuous Improvement

Cash flow management is not a one-time task—it's an ongoing process of evaluation and refinement. Establishing feedback loops ensures that you continuously improve your approach and adapt to changing market conditions.

Steps for Continuous Improvement:

1. **Regular Financial Reviews**: Analyze cash flow statements monthly or quarterly to identify trends or inefficiencies.

2. **Benchmarking**: Compare your portfolio's cash flow performance against market averages or similar properties to identify areas for improvement.
3. **Adjust Operating Budgets**: Revise budgets annually to reflect changes in income, expenses, or market conditions.

Tool Recommendation: Juniper Square offers portfolio-level reporting and benchmarking tools, allowing you to track performance and identify opportunities for improvement.

War Stories From the Alliance Vault:

The Compass and the Storm – How Sticking to My Principles Prevented Financial Ruin

In business, storms come in many forms. Some are financial, some are operational, and some are ethical. The hardest ones to navigate aren't always about numbers—they're about people. I've learned that no amount of money is worth it when you go against your core values. Two situations tested this principle, reaffirming a hard truth: Your compass is more important than the storm.

Story 1: The Investor Who Poisoned the Culture

There's an old saying that one bad apple can spoil the bunch. I learned this firsthand with an investor who, on paper, looked like a great asset to the company. But beneath the surface, he was a cancer to the culture.

It started as whispers. My male colleague's accountant was the first to raise the red flag. He had heard complaints from the Investor Relations team about how this investor treated the women in the company. At first, I listened but didn't act. Then, more stories surfaced. My team sat me down and shared the details:

- He made inappropriate remarks to the women on my team.
- He bullied staff members, putting them down to make himself feel superior.
- He would call just to complain, draining the energy from the team.
- My staff dreaded dealing with him, and it was affecting their ability to do their jobs.

This investor's money wasn't worth the damage he was doing to our environment. His work was toxic and shaped our culture in a way that went against everything I believed in. So, I made a decision: He had to go.

I removed him as an investor. His response? "Okay, fine."

My team's response? Relief. They were thrilled. It was a reminder that protecting culture is just as important as protecting capital. No individual or deal is worth sacrificing your principles.

Story 2: The Investor Relations Hire That Never Was

Hiring the right people is one of a leader's most important decisions. Just as the wrong investor can poison a culture, the wrong hire can do the same.

We were in the process of hiring someone for a key position in Investor Relations. He had the experience and credentials, and he looked like a great fit on paper. But one of my admin team members decided to dig deeper. She did some social media research—and what she found changed everything.

- *He was blatantly negative, attacking people online.*
- *His posts were racist, offensive, and degrading to women.*
- *His digital footprint showed exactly the kind of toxicity we wanted to avoid.*

I immediately revoked the offer. There was no second thought, no debate. Our core values weren't aligned; that was all I needed to know.

Could he have been great at his job? Maybe. But at what cost? You don't bring a problem into your house and hope it won't cause damage. That's not leadership—that's wishful thinking.

The Forgotten Scale: Balancing Risk and Reward

Both of these situations reminded me of one of the most fundamental principles in business and life:

- *When a relationship requires more time, energy, and effort than you get in return, it's time to walk away.*
- *It doesn't matter how great someone tries to paint the upside—if the present-day experience is a nightmare, that's the truth. You can't invest in what might be. You have to make decisions based on what is.*
- *You can't give more than you have to offer. And you can't take more than someone is willing to bring to the table.*

Lessons Learned: The Compass Over the Storm

1. Toxicity Spreads. One bad investor, one bad hire, or one bad relationship can have ripple effects that destroy a company's culture.
2. Your Core Values Are Non-Negotiable. If you compromise on them once, you'll do it again. And the cost will always be higher than the reward.

3. Money Isn't Everything. No amount of capital is worth sacrificing your principles. A toxic investor or employee will cost you more in the long run.
4. Do Your Homework. A little due diligence goes a long way. Social media, references, and gut checks matter. If someone's actions don't align with your company's values, walk away.
5. Don't Let People Sell You the Future. If they can't demonstrate value now, they won't magically create it later. Make decisions based on what exists—not what's promised.

Some storms test your finances. Others test your principles. I've survived both, and I can tell you this: Embedding your principles into the cornerstones of your **Hard Asset Empire™** will guide you to the right decisions every time.

Cornerstone Three Summary:

Cash flow discipline is the lifeblood and oxygen of your **Hard Asset Empire™**. You create a system that thrives in economic uncertainty by carefully evaluating income potential, controlling expenses, and maintaining liquidity. This third cornerstone ensures that you are prepared for challenges and positioned to capitalize on opportunities.

Success in cash flow management requires a combination of tools, strategies, and foresight. Platforms like **Stessa, Argus Enterprise**, and **ATOMIQ's nBrain** can streamline your efforts while disciplined financial practices provide the foundation for long-term growth. With these systems in place, you can ensure that your **Hard Asset Empire™** has the liquidity and stability needed to withstand hard times and seize the moments that matter. With discipline as your guide, your cash flow becomes more than a financial metric—it becomes the engine that powers your empire forward.

Cornerstone Four: Durability-Resilience Planning

In the unpredictable investing world, resilience is not just a desirable trait—it's a necessity. Building durability into your portfolio ensures that your investments can weather storms, recover from setbacks, and emerge stronger on the other side. Resilience planning is about anticipating challenges, stress-testing your strategy, and fortifying your portfolio against the inevitable economic shifts, regulatory changes, and market disruptions.

In the **Hard Asset Empire Blueprint™**, durability is the fourth and final cornerstone that separates fleeting success from enduring wealth. You can act decisively when others falter by proactively planning for downturns and creating systems to withstand volatility.

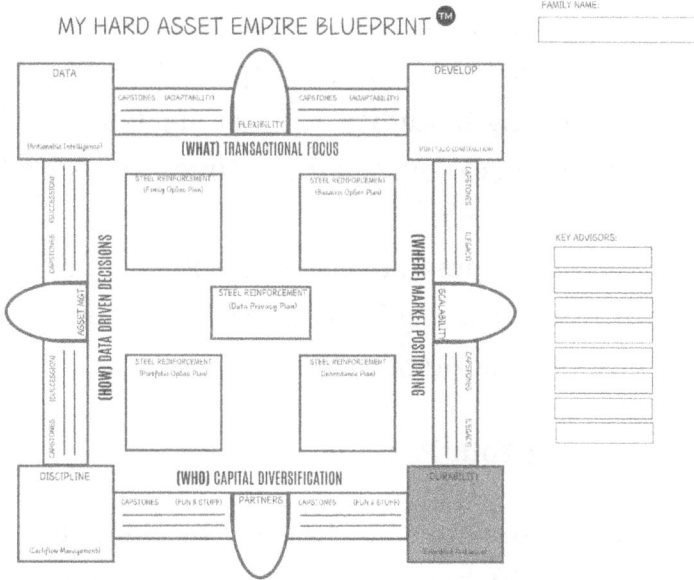

MY HARD ASSET EMPIRE BLUEPRINT ™

FAMILY NAME:

DATA

DEVELOP

FLEXIBILITY

(WHAT) TRANSACTIONAL FOCUS

KEY ADVISORS:

(HOW) DATA DRIVEN DECISIONS

(WHERE) MARKET POSITIONING

DISCIPLINE

(WHO) CAPITAL DIVERSIFICATION

DURABILITY

PARTNERS

Why Resilience Matters

Economic challenges are not hypothetical—they are a certainty. From interest rate hikes to tenant defaults, market downturns to regulatory changes, the potential obstacles facing investors are numerous and incessant. Resilience ensures that you are prepared for these events before they occur. It also allows you to shift from a defensive posture to an opportunistic one, turning crises into chances to grow your empire.

Key Benefits of Resilience Planning:

1. **Minimizing Losses**: By preparing for worst-case scenarios, you reduce the impact of economic shocks.
2. **Preserving Liquidity**: Maintaining financial flexibility allows you to navigate tough times without selling assets at a loss.
3. **Seizing Opportunities**: When others retreat, resilient investors can acquire distressed assets or secure advantageous terms.

Stress-Testing Your Portfolio

Resilience begins with understanding the vulnerabilities in your portfolio. Stress testing involves simulating adverse conditions to identify weaknesses and determine how your investments would perform under pressure.

How to Stress-Test Your Portfolio:

1. **Interest Rate Sensitivity**: Evaluate how rising interest rates would impact your cash flow and debt

servicing. For example, a 2% increase in interest rates could significantly raise costs for variable-rate loans.

2. **Occupancy Drops**: Analyze the effect of reduced occupancy rates on your properties. Consider scenarios where key tenants default or market demand declines.

3. **Market Corrections**: Assess the impact of a 20–30% drop in property values, particularly if you need to refinance or sell during a downturn.

4. **Expense Inflation**: Calculate how rising costs for maintenance, utilities, or property taxes would affect your NOI (net operating income).

Tool Recommendation: Use **Argus Enterprise** or **Trello for Real Estate Stress Testing** to model various scenarios and identify vulnerabilities in your portfolio.

Flexible Financing for Stability

Your financing strategy plays a critical role in resilience planning. Fixed-rate loans, long-term debt structures, and flexible financing options provide stability and adaptability.

Components of a Resilient Financing Strategy:

1. **Fixed-Rate Loans**: Locking in rates for the long term protects against sudden interest rate hikes.

2. **Debt Laddering**: Staggering loan maturities ensures you aren't forced to refinance multiple properties during a market downturn.
3. **Liquidity Buffers**: Maintain access to lines of credit or emergency funds to address short-term cash flow disruptions.
4. **Creative Financing**: Explore bridge loans, mezzanine debt, or joint ventures for flexibility in capital allocation.

Tool Recommendation: Platforms like **ATOMIQ's nBrain Tech** can help you manage financing structures and identify opportunities to optimize debt across your portfolio.

Maintaining Liquidity Reserves

Liquidity is the lifeline of a durable portfolio. In periods of uncertainty, having access to cash or easily liquidated assets ensures that you can meet obligations, capitalize on opportunities, and avoid selling long-term investments at unfavorable prices.

Guidelines for Liquidity Management:

1. **Emergency Reserves**: Keep at least 3–6 months of operating expenses for each property in cash reserves.

2. **Opportunity Funds**: Set aside funds specifically for acquiring distressed properties or expanding during downturns.
3. **Liquid Hard Assets**: Hold a portion (5-20%) of your portfolio in assets like gold or Bitcoin, which can be quickly converted to cash or borrowed against without selling the collateral.

Tool Recommendation: Use **Stessa** or **Personal Capital** to track liquidity across your portfolio and allocate reserves strategically.

Exit Strategies: Always Have a Plan B

In investing, flexibility is key. Multiple exit strategies ensure that you are never cornered into making decisions that harm your long-term goals. Whether it's selling an asset, refinancing a loan, or restructuring ownership, having options gives you control in turbulent times.

Common Exit Strategies:

1. **Refinancing**: Lock in better terms or free up equity during favorable market conditions.
2. **Asset Sales**: Sell properties in strong markets to realize gains or rebalance your portfolio.

3. **Joint Ventures**: Bring partners to share the financial burden and leverage their expertise.
4. **Buyouts**: Negotiate buyout options with partners or tenants for properties that no longer fit your strategy.

Tool Recommendation: Platforms like **CoStar, Crexi,** or **Reonomy** can provide market data to inform the timing and strategy for exits.

Building a Culture of Resilience

Durability is not just about preparing for downturns—it's about creating a mindset of adaptability and continuous improvement. A resilient investor embraces change, seeks knowledge, and builds systems that evolve with the market.

Steps to Build a Culture of Resilience:

1. **Ongoing Education**: Keep yourself and core team informed about market trends, regulatory changes, and emerging opportunities through resources like the **Alliance Intelligence Newsletter** at https://subscribetoben.com or the self-directed e-courses and deal-mentorship opportunities at Alliance Academy by visiting: https://www.alliancecgc.com/academy

2. **Regular Reviews**: Conduct quarterly reviews of portfolio performance and resilience metrics, adjusting strategies as needed.
3. **Team Collaboration**: Foster a team culture that values proactive problem-solving and encourages innovation in facing challenges.

Tool Recommendation: Trello or **Asana** can help manage team collaboration and track resilience planning tasks effectively.

Cornerstone Four Summary

Durability through resilience planning is the hallmark of a successful hard asset empire. By stress-testing your portfolio, maintaining flexible financing, building liquidity reserves, and crafting multiple exit strategies, you create a system capable of withstanding the inevitable challenges of investing.

The tools and strategies outlined here provide a framework for surviving and thriving during economic turbulence. Platforms like **Argus Enterprise**, **Juniper Square**, and **CoStar** offer actionable insights to optimize your resilience planning. With durability as your cornerstone, your investments are fortified and poised to grow, adapt, and create lasting wealth.

With resilience planning at the heart of your **Hard Asset Empire Blueprint™**, you can confidently face uncertainty, seize opportunities, and ensure your investments endure for generations. Resilience is also about mindset and a proof-point of your will. Those who panic during economic downturns often miss the opportunities that come with them. A well-prepared investor, by contrast, can act boldly, acquiring undervalued assets or renegotiating favorable terms. Durability ensures that you're not just surviving hard times but capitalizing on them.

Endnotes

1. CoStar Group, *Market Analysis and Trends*, https://www.costar.com/.
2. Skyline AI, *AI in Real Estate Investment*, https://www.skyline.ai/.
3. Tableau, *Data Visualization for Real Estate*, https://www.tableau.com/.
4. RealPage, *Real Estate Analytics*, https://www.realpage.com/.
5. Federal Reserve Economic Data (FRED), *Economic Indicators*, https://fred.stlouisfed.org/.
6. Yardi Matrix, *Multifamily Market Trends*, https://www.yardimatrix.com/.
7. Prophia, *Lease and Market Analytics*, https://www.prophia.com/.
8. Stessa, *Rental Property Financial Management*, https://www.stessa.com/.
9. Argus Enterprise, *Real Estate Valuation Software*, https://www.altusgroup.com/.
10. Buildium, *Property Management Software*, https://www.buildium.com/.
11. Yardi Breeze, *Expense Tracking for Real Estate*, https://www.yardibreeze.com/.
12. RealPage Portfolio Analytics, *Optimize Portfolio Performance*, https://www.realpage.com/.
13. Crexi, *Commercial Real Estate Listings*, https://www.crexi.com/.
14. Quicken for Real Estate, *Financial Software for Investors*, https://www.quicken.com/.
15. Juniper Square, *Portfolio Reporting and Analytics*, https://www.Junipersquare.com/.
16. Alliance Intelligence Newsletter, *Market Trends and Resilience Strategies*, https://subscribetoben.com/.

17. Reonomy, *Commercial Real Estate Intelligence*, https://www.reonomy.com/.
18. Trello, *Team Collaboration and Task Management*, https://www.trello.com/.
19. Personal Capital, *Liquidity Tracking and Planning*, https://www.personalcapital.com/.

4

Keystones - Holding Your Hard Asset Empire™ Together

Building a Hard Asset Empire™ isn't just about laying a strong foundation or erecting sturdy walls; it's about locking everything together to create stability, resilience, and adaptability. Keystones are the central elements that provide this cohesion. Just as architectural keystones hold an arch together, these investments and strategies ensure that your financial fortress is structurally sound, even under pressure. Without them, your empire risks fragmentation and instability.

In the context of a Hard Asset Empire™, keystones include **flexible deal structures**, **synergistic partnerships**, **integrated asset management**, and **scalable growth strategies**. These keystones unify your framework, providing the connectivity and adaptability necessary to thrive through economic cycles and market disruptions. This chapter dives deep into these elements, offering practical steps, insights, and tools to implement them effectively.

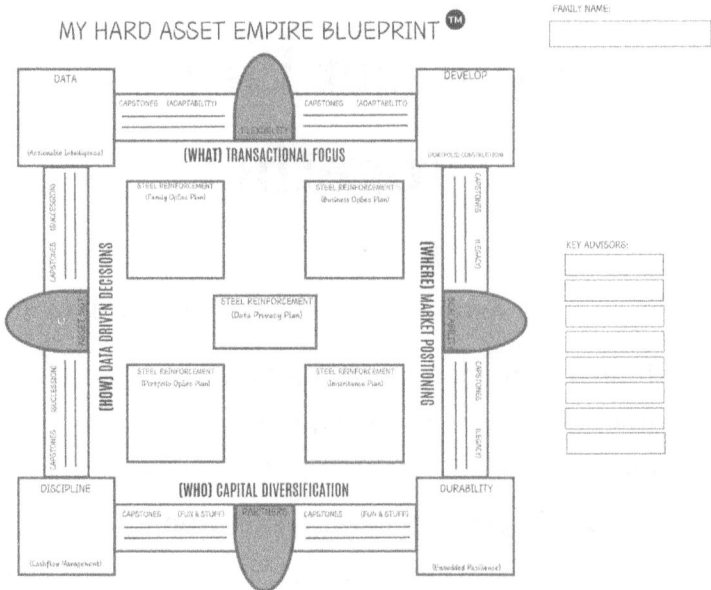

MY HARD ASSET EMPIRE BLUEPRINT™

Keystone One: Flexible Deal Structures-The Elasticity That Holds the System Together

Flexible deal structures are the mortar that adapts to shifts in your financial fortress. They provide the agility to navigate unpredictable economic conditions, project-specific challenges, and investor requirements while holding the entire system together. In an ever-changing market, rigidity can lead to cracks—whether through misaligned terms, unsustainable leverage, or inflexible commitments. Elasticity, on the other hand, gives you the freedom to pivot, adapt, and capitalize on opportunity without compromising the overall stability of your investments.

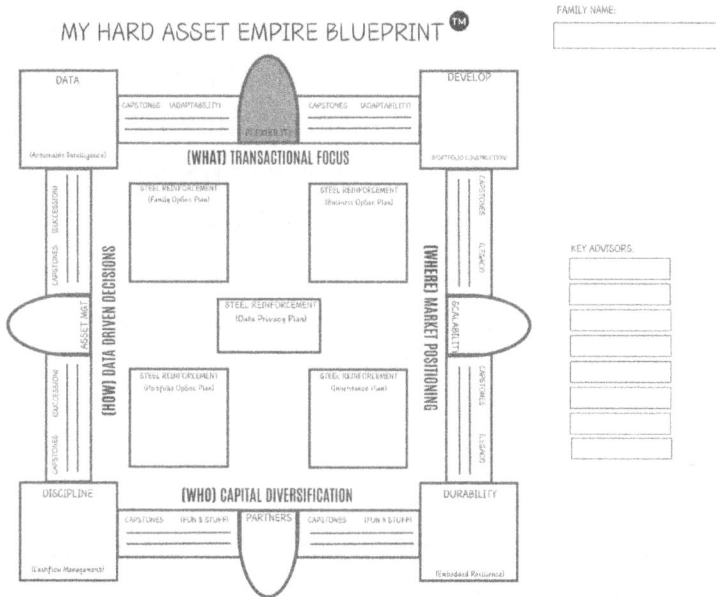

MY HARD ASSET EMPIRE BLUEPRINT™

Why Flexible Deal Structures Matter

Economic conditions constantly shift—interest rates rise, credit markets tighten, asset prices fluctuate, and buyer or tenant demand ebbs and flows. These shifts create volatility for investors, and those with rigid financial structures find themselves constrained, unable to weather external shocks or pivot to capitalize on opportunities. Flexible deal structures act as the shock absorbers of your financial fortress.

For instance, consider the recent market environment. With interest rates surging after a decade of near-zero borrowing costs, many investors locked into floating-rate loans were caught off guard by rising debt service obligations. Others, however, had structured deals with fixed-rate loans or had built-in contingencies to refinance or reposition when the environment changed. These investors maintained control, while others were forced into fire sales or distressed exits.

JVP Management's approach to the 96+Broadway project is a powerful example of how flexibility works in practice. By combining senior debt with mezzanine financing and equity sponsorship, they created a layered financial structure capable of absorbing risk while capturing upside potential. The senior debt provided stability and predictability, while the mezzanine and equity components allowed them to generate additional returns without excessive exposure. This ability to align financing structures with a project's unique requirements distinguishes successful, resilient investors from those who falter.

How to Build Flexibility Into Your Portfolio

Building flexibility into your portfolio requires intention, strategy, and access to diverse financial tools. The goal is to create deal structures that are tailored to each project, adaptive to shifting conditions, and resilient to unforeseen challenges. Below are practical steps to integrate flexibility into your approach:

1. **Diversify Your Financing Tools**
   Successful investors cultivate various funding sources to remain agile across different market cycles. Develop relationships with traditional banks, private lenders, institutional equity investors, and alternative capital providers like family offices or debt funds. When one source becomes constrained, multiple options ensure you can still close deals and remain in control.

   - **Traditional Financing:** Banks and credit unions offer cost-effective capital for stabilized assets.

- **Alternative Debt:** Mezzanine financing, bridge loans, or asset-based lending can fill funding gaps.
- **Private Equity and Syndications:** Partnering with equity investors reduces your capital exposure while sharing the rewards of growth.

2. **Customize Each Structure for the Specific Deal**
No two deals are the same; your financing approach shouldn't be either. Some projects may benefit from senior debt with a lower cost of capital, while others may require a hybrid structure with equity participation. Consider options like delayed draw loans or construction financing that align with project milestones for value-added projects. For stabilized assets, long-term fixed-rate financing may provide predictable cash flow.

3. **Model Multiple Scenarios**
Financial modeling is critical to testing the resilience of your deal structures. Tools like **Altus Group** allow you to run multiple "what-if" scenarios—testing assumptions around interest rates, rental income, and capital expenditures. Scenario modeling helps you identify vulnerabilities in a proposed deal structure

and prepare contingency plans.

4. **Retain Optionality Wherever Possible**
   Avoid overly rigid agreements that could limit your ability to pivot in response to challenges when negotiating terms. Key elements of optionality include:

   - Prepayment Flexibility: Avoid loans with heavy penalties for early repayment.
   - Refinancing Windows: Structure loans with opportunities to refinance or reposition midway through the project.
   - Partner Agreements: Negotiate exit clauses that allow flexibility to bring in additional partners or repurchase equity stakes.

5. **Leverage Cutting-Edge Tools and Technology**
   AI-driven platforms have revolutionized deal structuring by combining real-time market intelligence with predictive analytics. For instance, **ATOMIQ nBrain™** integrates financial modeling with actionable intelligence, allowing you to adapt deal structures dynamically in response to shifting conditions. This tool connects internal and external data feeds, helping investors identify financing

opportunities, stress-test structures, and align terms with project performance.

Practical Example: A Layered Deal in Action

Imagine acquiring a 100,000-square-foot industrial property in a growing logistics hub. A flexible deal structure might include:

- **Senior Debt:** A traditional 65% loan-to-value (LTV) mortgage from a regional bank at a fixed rate for five years, ensuring predictable debt service.
- **Mezzanine Financing:** A secondary loan covering an additional 10% of the capital stack to reduce equity exposure and improve cash-on-cash returns.
- **Equity Investment:** A joint venture partner provides the final 25%, sharing risk and reward while reducing capital requirements.
- **Optional Refinancing Clause:** After stabilizing the property, you can refinance at a lower interest rate or withdraw additional equity to redeploy elsewhere.

This layered structure provides stability, enhances returns, and allows for flexibility in pivoting or optimizing as market conditions evolve.

Recommended Tools for Flexible Deal Structuring

1. **Altus Group**: Industry-standard financial modeling and scenario analysis software.
2. **Dealpath**: A deal pipeline and transaction management tool for streamlined oversight.
3. **ATOMIQ nBrain™**: An open-source Enterprise AI-Agent platform integrating real-time intelligence with dynamic deal structuring capabilities.

Keystone One Summary:

Flexible deal structures are the glue that holds your Hard Asset Empire™ together. They connect your foundational principles with strategy's cornerstones and ensure that your portfolio remains agile, resilient, and adaptable. By diversifying financing tools, customizing structures for each deal, and leveraging cutting-edge technology, you can protect yourself against market volatility while maximizing your ability to capitalize on new opportunities.

In a market where the rules constantly shift, elasticity isn't optional—it's essential. A rigid structure might stand for a while but it will crack under pressure. Flexible deal structures allow your financial fortress to absorb shocks, adapt seamlessly, and grow stronger. Now you can connect your Hard Asset Empire™ to the ecosystem through **synergistic partnerships.**

Keystone Two: Synergistic Partnerships-The Fasteners Binding Your Empire

If flexible deal structures are the mortar adapting to market shifts, synergistic partnerships are the fasteners that bind your financial fortress together. These partnerships—whether with brokers, lenders, developers, corporate anchors, tenants, or service providers—serve as the screws, bolts, and nails that connect every part of your empire. They ensure cohesion, strength, and the ability to adapt as your portfolio grows. Without these fasteners, even the most well-planned foundations, cornerstones, and keystones risk becoming disjointed, weakening your entire Hard Asset Empire™.

MY HARD ASSET EMPIRE BLUEPRINT ™

FAMILY NAME:

DATA   DEVELOP

CAPSTONES (ADAPTABILITY)   CAPSTONES (ADAPTABILITY)

FLEXIBILITY

(Actionable Intelligence)   **(WHAT) TRANSACTIONAL FOCUS**   (Portfolio Construction)

STEEL REINFORCEMENT (Family OpSec Plan)

STEEL REINFORCEMENT (Universe OpSec Plan)

(HOW) DATA DRIVEN DECISIONS   ASSET MGT   SUCCESSION   CAPSTONES

STEEL REINFORCEMENT (Data Privacy Plan)

(WHERE) MARKET POSITIONING   SCALABILITY   LEGACY   CAPSTONES

STEEL REINFORCEMENT (Portfolio OpSec Plan)

STEEL REINFORCEMENT (Inheritance Plan)

DISCIPLINE   **(WHO) CAPITAL DIVERSIFICATION**   DURABILITY

CAPSTONES (FUN & STUFF)   PARTNERS   CAPSTONES (FUN & STUFF)

(Cashflow Management)   (Embodied Resilience)

FAMILY NAME:

KEY ADVISORS:

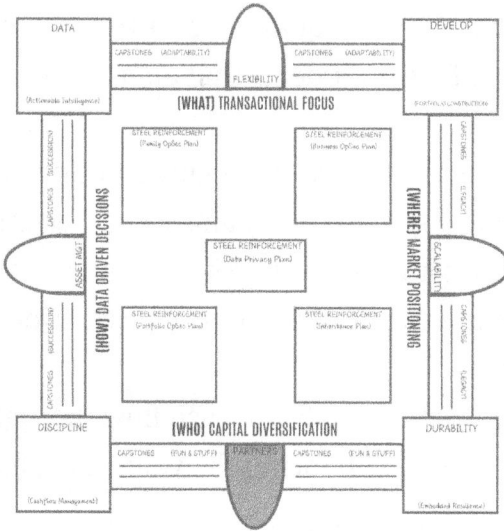

The Role of Synergistic Partnerships

Fasteners do more than hold individual elements together — they create a system of interconnected strength that multiplies your capacity, mitigates risk, and opens doors to new opportunities. These partnerships enable you to leverage external expertise, share the workload, and extend your reach.

Each partnership plays a specific role:

- **Brokers** uncover high-quality opportunities, often identifying off-market deals that align with your strategy.
- **Lenders** provide creative financing solutions tailored to your project's unique challenges and objectives.
- **Developers** bring local expertise, helping to expedite zoning approvals and streamline construction management.
- **Corporate anchors** stabilize cash flow through long-term leases, enhancing the value and appeal of your properties.
- **Tenants** ensure consistent income streams, which serve as the lifeblood of your portfolio.
- **Service providers** such as property managers, insurance brokers, and maintenance teams keep operations running smoothly.

For example, a strategically chosen corporate anchor like a logistics firm in an industrial warehouse can boost property valuation, stabilize income, and make the asset more attractive to future investors. Similarly, a partnership with a knowledgeable local developer can transform a challenging project into a seamless process by navigating zoning laws, permitting, and contractor relationships.

Building Your Partnership Ecosystem

Building a network of trusted, aligned partners is like assembling a toolkit of fasteners tailored to your specific needs. Each type of partner contributes unique value to your **Hard Asset Empire™**.

Brokers and Bird Dogs: Scouts for Opportunities

Brokers and bird dogs are your front-line scouts, connecting you to high-value opportunities. Brokers bring industry expertise, market data, and an expansive network, while bird dogs operate in niche spaces, often uncovering hidden gems.

Action Steps:

- Build long-term relationships with brokers who specialize in your target markets.
- Use platforms like **Crexi** and **CoStar** to access a pipeline of deals and connect with market experts.
- Establish clear incentive programs for bird dogs, rewarding them for bringing high-quality deals to your attention.

Lenders and Sponsors: Financial Fasteners

Lenders and sponsors provide the financial resources that connect your capital needs with growth opportunities. Banks, private equity firms, and family offices offer diverse financing options to match your project's scope and risk profile.

Action Steps:

- Diversify your network to include traditional lenders, private credit funds, and patient capital sources like family offices.
- Leverage equity sponsors who can share the financial burden and align with your long-term objectives.
- Use tools like **Juniper Square** to ensure financial transparency and manage equity contributions effectively.

Tenants and Anchors: Stabilizing Fasteners

Tenants, especially corporate anchors, stabilize cash flow and enhance property value. For commercial real estate, securing financially strong tenants is essential to minimizing vacancies and ensuring steady income.

Action Steps:

- Partner with corporate tenants or anchors whose business models align with long-term market trends. Logistics firms, healthcare providers, and technology companies are strong candidates.
- Use tenant management tools like **Buildium** to improve tenant satisfaction and retention rates for multifamily properties.
- Proactively build relationships with tenants to anticipate their future needs and maintain high occupancy rates.

Service Providers: Operational Fasteners

Service providers keep the operational components of your empire connected. From property managers to insurance brokers, these partners ensure that your properties perform at their peak while mitigating risks.

Action Steps:

- Vet service providers based on their track record, reliability, and expertise in managing similar assets.
- Integrate providers into a centralized communication system to avoid silos and inefficiencies.

- Regularly review contracts and performance to ensure alignment with your evolving goals.

Practical Steps for Effective Partnership Management

1. **Define Clear Objectives:**
   Outline the roles and goals for each partnership. Misaligned objectives weaken the fasteners and reduce the effectiveness of your ecosystem.

2. **Leverage Technology:**
   Platforms like **Juniper Square** and **Buildium** streamline partnership operations by providing centralized data management, transparency, and communication tools.

3. **Expand Your Network:**
   Attend industry conferences, join professional organizations, and actively use tools like **Crexi** to connect with brokers, lenders, and other critical partners.

4. **Create Incentives:**
   Incentivize brokers, bird dogs, and other stakeholders to ensure that everyone's efforts align.

Recommended Tools for Partnership Ecosystem Management

- **Crexi:** A platform for sourcing deals and connecting with brokers.
- **CoStar:** Comprehensive market analytics and property intelligence.
- **Juniper Square:** Streamlines equity partnerships and investor relations.
- **Buildium:** Simplifies tenant and property management.

The Long-Term Benefits of Synergistic Partnerships

Strong fasteners transform your financial fortress into an interconnected system of resilience and opportunity. Synergistic partnerships ensure that every component—whether an individual asset, financing solution, or operational team—works harmoniously toward the same objectives.

These partnerships enhance your ability to scale efficiently, weather economic storms, and seize opportunities that would be impossible to capture alone. You create a network that strengthens your portfolio's stability and adaptability by building a robust ecosystem of brokers, lenders, tenants, developers, and service providers.

In construction, the integrity of a structure depends on the strength of its fasteners. Similarly, in the world of hard asset investing, your partnerships' strength determines your empire's durability and scalability. By prioritizing aligned goals, leveraging technology, and continuously expanding your network, you ensure that the fasteners holding your Hard Asset Empire™ together are resilient and effective.

Keystone Two Summary

Synergistic partnerships are the fasteners that secure every aspect of your Hard Asset Empire™, ensuring that all components remain connected and aligned. From brokers scouting opportunities to tenants stabilizing cash flow and service providers managing day-to-day operations, these partnerships multiply value, reduce risk, and enable growth.

You create an adaptable and resilient system by taking a strategic approach to partnership management—building relationships, leveraging technology, and aligning goals.

With these fasteners in place, your financial fortress is well-built and primed for enduring success.

The next section will explore **Keystone Three: Integrated Asset Management**. This nervous system ensures every part of your empire communicates and operates in alignment with your long-term vision.

Keystone Three: Integrated Asset Management
-Connecting Operations to Strategy and Harnessing Actionable Intelligence

Just as nerves transmit signals between the brain and the body to maintain balance and control, integrated asset management connects the day-to-day operations of your portfolio to your strategic objectives. Without this vital system, even the most carefully constructed portfolio can falter under inefficiencies, missed opportunities, or misaligned goals. Integrated asset management ensures your assets function optimally and contribute meaningfully to the overarching growth and resilience of your **Hard Asset Empire™**.

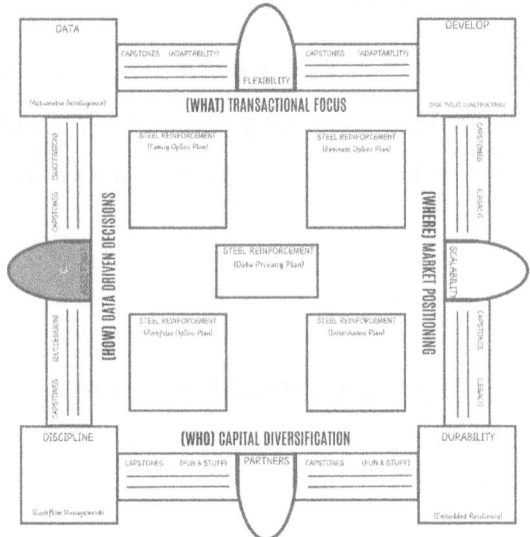

MY HARD ASSET EMPIRE BLUEPRINT ™

FAMILY NAME:

DATA

DEVELOP

FLEXIBILITY

(WHAT) TRANSACTIONAL FOCUS

KEY ADVISORS:

(HOW) DATA DRIVEN DECISIONS

(WHERE) MARKET POSITIONING

STEEL REINFORCEMENT

DISCIPLINE

(WHO) CAPITAL DIVERSIFICATION

DURABILITY

PARTNERS

The Importance of Integration

Many investors focus heavily on acquisitions, believing that the strength of their portfolio lies solely in the quality of their assets. However, the operational performance of these assets is just as critical. Poorly managed properties, delayed maintenance, or disorganized financial tracking can erode tenant satisfaction, reduced net operating income (NOI), and depreciated asset values.

Integration bridges the gap between strategy and execution by ensuring that every property in your portfolio is aligned with your financial goals and operating at peak efficiency. It centralizes data, simplifies processes, and provides actionable insights that allow you to act quickly and decisively when opportunities or challenges arise.

For instance, consider a mixed-use property with retail tenants. If tenant feedback about maintenance delays or unfulfilled requests goes unnoticed, dissatisfaction grows, leases are not renewed, and income drops. With integrated asset management, such issues can be flagged early, enabling proactive solutions that maintain tenant retention and cash flow.

How RAG Model AI Platforms Like ATOMIQ's nBrain™ Revolutionize Asset Management

Modern integrated asset management systems are no longer just about spreadsheets and manual oversight. The rise of AI and tools like ATOMIQ's nBrain™ introduces a transformative approach: Retrieval-Augmented Generation (RAG) model AI systems. These systems act as a centralized "switching station" for intelligence, seamlessly integrating data from multiple sources, automating workflows, and enabling predictive analytics.

Centralized Intelligence

Open-source RAG model AI-agent platforms like nBrain™ can be customized into your proprietary asset management platform, like the one we built with *Alliance REI Nexus*. This platform uses data from disparate sources, including property management software, financial systems, tenant communication platforms, and external market data providers like CoStar or Reonomy. By centralizing this data, our Alliance REI Nexus powered by nBrain™ creates a unified dashboard that provides real-time insights into the portfolio's performance.

Example:
A multifamily investor managing properties across different states can use nBrain™ to monitor occupancy rates, tenant feedback, and real-time maintenance requests. If occupancy in one building begins to dip, the system can automatically flag the issue, identify patterns in tenant turnover, and suggest corrective actions such as targeted marketing campaigns or rent adjustments.

Streamlined Standard Operating Procedures

RAG model AI excels at automating and standardizing routine processes, saving time and reducing human error. With customized enterprise AI agents, you can automate lease management, generate financial reports, maintenance alerts, upcoming lease renewals, off-market and on-market offer letter generation, and even handle tenant inquiries through intelligent chat interfaces.

Example:
In a large commercial property, you could automatically schedule preventive maintenance based on equipment usage patterns and track vendor performance. At the same time, it could review lease renewal timelines and notify property managers of upcoming expirations, ensuring no lease slips through the cracks.

Actionable Insights and Predictive Analytics

RAG systems go beyond descriptive data to provide predictive and prescriptive insights. They can analyze historical trends, model future scenarios, and recommend specific actions to improve portfolio performance.

Example:
For a medical office building, you might analyze regional healthcare demand trends and recommend adjustments to tenant mix to attract high-demand specialties. It could also flag opportunities to renegotiate lease terms with existing tenants based on market dynamics.

Securing Proprietary Data

With tools like nBrain™, you maintain control over your proprietary data and operating procedures while agnostically leveraging the best emerging AI infrastructure or third-party widgets and data sources. This is particularly important as AI systems rely on large language models (LLMs) and third-party tools and are evolving more rapidly than any other technology in the history of humanity. Building on top of a code base like nBrain™ ensures that your data remains protected and owned by you and that you don't have to start over when the AI arms race of large infrastructure players disrupt one another with better, more efficient models. while still leveraging the best in class from LLM providers like OpenAI, LLama, DeepSeek, or Anthropic, to name a few. Think of it like when you wire a building for electricity, you wanna make sure that regardless of your utility provider, you don't have to rip open the walls and rewire every time you change power companies.

Steps to Implement Integrated Asset Management

1. Centralize Data and Systems

The first step is consolidating operational, financial, and performance data into a single platform. Platforms like Yardi Voyager or RealPage can provide this functionality, but integrating them with an enterprise AI tool like nBrain™ elevates their utility by synthesizing disparate datasets into actionable intelligence.

2. Define Key Performance Indicators (KPIs)

Establish clear KPIs that align with your strategic goals. Common metrics include:

- Net Operating Income (NOI)
- Occupancy and retention rates
- Tenant satisfaction scores
- Cash-on-cash return. These KPIs should be real-time monitored to identify trends and inform decision-making.

3. Automate Processes

Use AI to automate repetitive tasks such as lease renewals, maintenance scheduling, and financial reporting. This improves efficiency and frees up time for high-value activities like strategy development and deal sourcing.

4. Foster Team Alignment

Ensure that all stakeholders—property managers, accountants, and asset managers—work toward shared objectives. Use collaborative platforms like Prophia or Buildium to streamline communication and foster team transparency.

5. Harness Predictive Analytics

Deploy AI tools to model future scenarios and proactively address potential challenges. For example, predictive analytics can forecast how interest rate changes might impact your cash flow or identify assets at risk of underperformance.

Recommended Tools for Integrated Asset Management

1. ATOMIQ's nBrain™: A customizable RAG model AI platform that centralizes intelligence, automates workflows, and generates actionable insights. Ideal for

managing portfolios of $500M AUM or more. ***Full disclosure:*** *Alliance has been building its Alliance Intelligence division and customized proprietary suite of AI powered tools like Alliance REI Nexus on this platform.*

2. Yardi Voyager:
   A comprehensive property management system that consolidates data and simplifies operations for large portfolios.

3. Prophia:
   Focused on lease analytics, Prophia helps uncover trends and opportunities across commercial assets.

4. Buildium:
   Streamlines tenant management and operational efficiency for smaller-scale investors.

Long-Term Benefits of Integrated Asset Management

Integrated asset management transforms your portfolio from a collection of properties into a unified, intelligent system.

Aligning daily operations with strategic objectives ensures that each asset contributes to your long-term goals.

Case Study

An investor managing a mixed portfolio of industrial and multifamily properties implemented AI to consolidate data from property management systems, market research platforms, and tenant communication tools. The AI identified inefficiencies in utility expenses across their multifamily holdings and recommended switching vendors, resulting in a 12% cost reduction. Simultaneously, the system flagged an industrial property nearing lease expiration and suggested market-aligned rent adjustments, boosting NOI by 8%.

Keystone Three Summary:

Integrated asset management is your Hard Asset Empire™ nerve center, ensuring that operations align seamlessly with strategy. Tools like ATOMIQ's nBrain™ provide the connective tissue needed to harness intelligence, automate processes, and optimize performance. By centralizing data, defining clear KPIs, and leveraging predictive analytics, you create a system capable of responding to challenges and seizing opportunities in real time.

The next section will explore Scalable Growth Strategies, the adhesive connectors that enable controlled expansion and sustained success. Together, these elements ensure that your financial fortress remains strong, cohesive, and adaptable to the demands of the modern investment landscape. Now you are ready for the last keystone of **scalable growth strategies**.

Keystone Four: Scalable Growth Strategies - The Adhesive Connectors That Enable Expansion

In any structure, adhesive connectors create the secure, flexible bonds that allow for expansion without compromising integrity. They ensure that new elements fit seamlessly into the existing framework, reinforcing the whole system rather than weakening it. Similarly, scalable growth strategies are the adhesive connectors of your Hard Asset Empire™, enabling controlled and intentional growth while preserving the stability of your foundational investments.

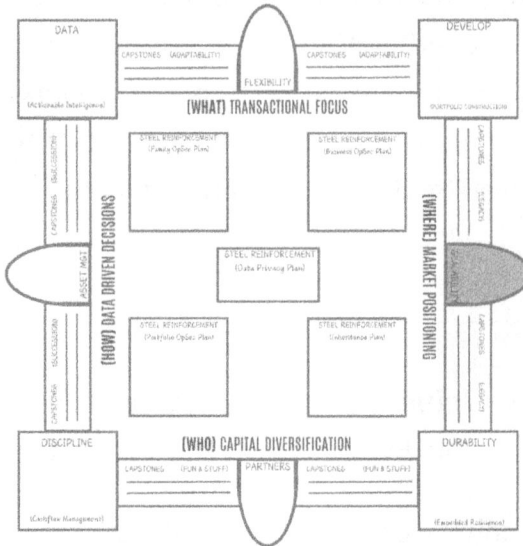

MY HARD ASSET EMPIRE BLUEPRINT ™

FAMILY NAME:

DATA

DEVELOP

CAPSTONES (ADAPTABILITY)   CAPSTONES (ADAPTABILITY)

FLEXIBILITY

(Actionable Intelligence)

[WHAT] TRANSACTIONAL FOCUS

PORTFOLIO CONSTRUCTION

STEEL REINFORCEMENT
(Family Office Plan)

STEEL REINFORCEMENT
(Business Option Plan)

[HOW] DATA DRIVEN DECISIONS

[WHERE] MARKET POSITIONING

STEEL REINFORCEMENT
(Data Privacy Plan)

STEEL REINFORCEMENT
(Portfolio Option Plan)

STEEL REINFORCEMENT
(Inheritance Plan)

KEY ADVISORS:

DISCIPLINE

[WHO] CAPITAL DIVERSIFICATION

DURABILITY

CAPSTONES (RUN A STORE)   PARTNERS   CAPSTONES (RUN A STORE)

(Cashflow Management)

(Compound Resilience)

The Principles of Scalable Growth

Scalable growth is not about reckless expansion—it's about replicating success to enhance your portfolio's overall resilience and performance. Without careful planning, expansion can lead to overexposure, misaligned investments, or operational inefficiencies. By focusing on replicable processes, strategic diversification, and efficient capital recycling, you can ensure that growth is both sustainable and profitable.

1. **Replication of Proven Models**

   Growth begins with identifying what works. Whether it's a specific asset class, market, or management approach, the strategies that deliver consistent returns can often be scaled to new opportunities. For example, if multifamily investments in secondary markets have yielded strong cash flow, expanding into similar markets with comparable demographics and economic conditions is a logical next step. Replicating proven models reduces risk and increases the likelihood of success.

2. **Geographic Diversification**

   Expanding into new regions allows you to hedge against local market risks while capturing opportunities in emerging areas. Demographic shifts, economic growth, and favorable regulatory environments all contribute to identifying viable markets. Tools like **CoStar** and **Reonomy** provide detailed market intelligence, helping you assess potential locations and asset classes.

3. **Capital Recycling**

   One of the most effective ways to fund growth is through capital recycling. You create a self-sustaining growth cycle by reinvesting profits from stabilized assets or executing strategic sales. For instance, selling a fully leased office building in a mature market could fund the acquisition of a value-added multifamily property in an up-and-coming area. This approach ensures that your empire expands without overleveraging or depleting reserves.

Steps to Building Scalable Strategies

1. Evaluate Market Conditions

Growth opportunities must be rooted in data. Tools like **CoStar** offer comprehensive market analysis, allowing you to identify regions with favorable trends such as population growth, job creation, and infrastructure development. Look for markets where demand outpaces supply, as these conditions often yield the highest returns.

2. Develop Repeatable Processes

Standardization is key to scalability. To streamline operations and reduce inefficiencies, create consistent processes for acquisitions, financing, and management. Documenting best practices and using technology to automate routine tasks ensures that growth does not strain existing resources.

3. Diversify Asset Classes

Diversification goes beyond geographic regions. Expanding into complementary asset classes allows you to build a portfolio that thrives under various market conditions. For example:

- **Multifamily properties** provide stable cash flow during economic downturns.
- **Industrial assets** capitalize on the growth of e-commerce and logistics.
- **Medical office buildings** benefit from inelastic demand for healthcare services.
- **Alternative assets** like Bitcoin or gold offer liquidity and protection against inflation.

4. Leverage Technology for Expansion

Scalable growth requires systems that can handle increased complexity. Platforms like **RealPage Portfolio Analytics** help track performance across an expanding portfolio, while tools like **Juniper Square** provide centralized management for equity partnerships and investor relations.

5. Create Growth Contingency Plans

Even the best-laid growth strategies face unforeseen challenges. Develop contingency plans for potential setbacks, such as market downturns or financing delays. Maintaining liquidity reserves and aligning with flexible lenders ensures you can pivot when necessary.

Case Study: A Strategic Growth Pathway

An investor with a successful portfolio of multifamily properties in the Midwest might decide to diversify into industrial warehouses in the Southeast, a region experiencing a boom in logistics-driven demand. The investor identifies an underdeveloped industrial corridor with high potential by leveraging relationships with existing lenders and using tools like **CoStar** for market analysis.

Using a combination of profits from stabilized multifamily assets and additional mezzanine financing, the investor acquires and upgrades a series of warehouses, securing long-term leases with established logistics firms. The expansion diversifies the portfolio and positions it for growth in a sector aligned with macroeconomic trends.

Recommended Tools for Scalable Growth

- **CoStar**: Comprehensive market analysis and forecasting tool to identify growth opportunities.
- **Reonomy**: A commercial real estate intelligence platform for uncovering new markets and properties.
- **RealPage Portfolio Analytics**: Tracks portfolio performance, providing insights into areas for growth.
- **Altus Group**: Offers scenario analysis to evaluate the impact of growth initiatives on your overall strategy.

Keystone Four Summary:

Scalable growth strategies are not about adding assets haphazardly—they are about thoughtful, intentional expansion that aligns with your long-term vision. Like adhesive connectors in construction, these strategies ensure that new components integrate seamlessly with existing ones, creating a unified and resilient whole.

By embracing scalable growth principles—replicating success, diversifying geographically and across asset classes, recycling capital, and leveraging technology—you position your Hard Asset Empire™ for sustained success. Growth becomes a mechanism for reinforcing stability, not compromising it.

With the right tools and strategies in place, your empire is poised to expand while maintaining the structural integrity needed to endure economic storms and capitalize on opportunities. In the next chapter, we'll explore Incremental Growth Assets—the bricks and mortar that add layers of strength and durability to your fortress, ensuring its continued evolution and resilience.

The Glue That Holds It All Together

Scalable growth strategies ensure that your financial fortress doesn't just remain static—it evolves, expands, and strengthens over time. These strategies are the adhesive connectors that bond new acquisitions, processes, and markets to your existing portfolio, creating a cohesive and resilient empire.

The key to successful expansion lies in balancing ambition with caution. By replicating proven models, diversifying strategically, and leveraging technology, you can achieve growth that enhances rather than destabilizes your Hard Asset Empire™. Each new acquisition, market entry, or strategic partnership becomes another strength layer in a structure designed to endure.

Summary:

The keystones—**Flexibility** (flexible deal structures), **Partners** (synergistic partnerships), **Asset Management** (integrated asset management), and **Scalability** (scalable growth strategies)—are the elements that hold your financial fortress together. They are the connections, the glue, and the mechanisms that ensure your Hard Asset Empire™ is resilient, adaptable, and primed for continuous growth. Each keystone serves a unique purpose: flexible deal structures allow you to adapt to shifting conditions, synergistic partnerships expand your capabilities, integrated asset management aligns operations with strategy, and scalable growth strategies enable measured and intentional expansion.

Without these keystones, even the strongest foundations and cornerstones can falter under pressure. But when implemented effectively, they ensure that every part of your financial fortress works in harmony, creating a structure that not only withstands economic challenges but thrives in their wake.

This is not about building a scattered collection of assets. It's about creating a cohesive, interconnected empire that can endure, adapt, and grow for generations to come. By mastering these keystone strategies and leveraging the recommended tools, you will have the framework and systems to solidify your Hard Asset Empire™, turning ambition into enduring wealth.

In the next chapter, we'll shift our focus to **Incremental Growth Assets**—the bricks and mortar that add layers of strength and durability to your fortress, ensuring that it continues to evolve while maintaining structural integrity.

War Stories from the Alliance Vault:

Story 1: Betting the House on Bitcoin – My Journey from Doubt to Generational Wealth

*Every investor faces a moment when they're forced to rethink everything they know. For me, that moment came with **Bitcoin**. At first, I dismissed it. It sounded like a passing trend, an experiment for tech geeks, not a real asset class. But as I would soon learn, ignoring Bitcoin wasn't an option—it was showing up everywhere in my life, and the more I investigated, the more undeniable it became.*

The First Encounter: A Skeptic's Introduction

*I first heard about **Bitcoin** in **Chicago**, when a local service provider started accepting it as payment. It was an interesting concept, but I didn't give it much thought. Then a close friend sat me down and walked me through the basics. **He helped me set up my first Coinbase account.** It felt experimental, almost like a game—but that game would soon become much bigger.*

*At the same time, my son **Joey** was taking a class that introduced him to blockchain technology. As he learned, I learned. I started to understand that **blockchain wasn't just about Bitcoin—it was a fundamental shift in how value and ownership worked.** That's when I began investing not just in Bitcoin itself but in the infrastructure surrounding it.*

The Turning Point: Trump and the Future of Bitcoin

*Joey and I traveled to **Nashville,** where we attended a speech by **Donald Trump**. His speech about **Bitcoin and its role in the future financial system** struck a chord with me. I had already begun exploring blockchain solutions for **Alliance and our investors**, which solidified it. If Bitcoin were part of the future economy, it must be part of my investment strategy.*

*Soon after, I interviewed a **Bitcoin investor who was in the process of acquiring a bank (Signature Bank)** on my podcast.*

His insights reinforced everything I had learned: **the old financial system was vulnerable, and blockchain was the next frontier.**

Books, Strategies, and the Bigger Picture

The deeper I dug, the more convinced I became. Books like Read Write Own by Chris Dixon explained the transition from traditional internet models (read-only) to Web3 (read, write, and own). The concept of owning digital assets rather than just participating in financial systems controlled by intermediaries was powerful. It wasn't just about money—it was about freedom.

At the same time, I was working on a real estate liquidation deal with James, and I started seeing how Bitcoin could play a role in alternative financing, collateralization, and liquidity solutions for investors.

Bitcoin had gone from a speculative incremental growth asset to a Scalable Growth Strategy Keystone in my wealth strategy.

Story 2: The Flexible Deal Structure Keystone That Catapulted My Fortune

This wasn't the first time I had made a bold move in investing. Years earlier, I had faced another pivotal moment with a **commercial property in Libertyville, IL.**

At the time, the economy was struggling. *I acquired a building at a steep discount from an attorney struggling to plug a financial hole on another project in his portfolio.* The existing tenant was a successful and growing orthopoedic practice that was investing heavily in custom tenant improvements and had acquired the adjacent building next door as part of their expansion, but had forgotten to exercise their option to extend their current lease another five years, so my property was coming up for a total lease renewal.

The **property association** added another layer of complexity, making it difficult for the tenant to make modifications outside of their footprint. And yet, **their lease was about to expire.** They had no real leverage if they wanted to continue to operate their business out of this recently customized space.

This gave me the opportunity to create a long-term (15-year) lease with a tenant whose credit was improving, and who was financially and emotionally trapped to renew a long-term lease with me because they had just invested so much hard cost in the office space. The creative solution that my property management arm and I negotiated to improve the value of this asset, has become known now as the "Alliance Clause" because it required them to report their financial statements each year as part of the 15-year lease which improved the property's lending profile with my banks and the investment community.

The Power of Leverage

Because I held the leverage, we secured:

- ***A 10% rent bump***
- ***A long-term lease with 3% annual escalations***
- ***Financial transparency from the tenant*** *(which we later coined as the "Alliance Clause")*
- ***The realization that they had purchased the building next door meant their expansion was tied to staying put and accepting my lease terms or buying me out for the space they just improved, which I now owned.***

*It turned into a **home run deal**. When we sold, we delivered **a significant total return of 338% (an IRR 34%) to our investors**, reinforcing **Alliance's reputation for structuring deals that maximize value.***

Lessons Learned in this Chapter:

These experiences taught me some of the most important reasons for having these keystones in your Hard Asset Empire™ Blueprint:

1. **Don't Dismiss Innovation Too Early.** Bitcoin went from a curiosity to **a building block of my portfolio.**

Just because something is unfamiliar doesn't mean it's not valuable.

2. **Hold Your Ground.** In real estate and investing, **leverage is everything.** If I had caved to the tenant in Libertyville, I would have lost millions in future value.

3. **Do Your Homework.** Whether it's blockchain or a lease negotiation, **understanding the details gives you the edge.** The more I learned about Bitcoin, the more I saw its inevitability.

4. **Creating Win-Win Deals Is the Goal.** My job as an investor isn't to squeeze the other side—it's to make a deal that maximizes value for **everyone involved.**

5. **The Ability to Hold Determines Success.** Whether it's holding real estate through a tough market or holding Bitcoin through price volatility, **the investors who win are the ones who don't panic.**

My Prediction For the Future

Bitcoin started as a small curiosity, just like my Libertyville deal began as a small opportunity. But both turned into defining moments of my career.

The best investments don't always look obvious at first. But if you understand leverage, do your research, and play the long game, you'll be ahead of the curve every time.

The keystone of high-impact investing isn't chasing trends—it's knowing when to stand your ground and **when to bet the house.**

Endnotes

1. Altus Group, *Real Estate Valuation Software*, https://www.altusgroup.com/.
2. Dealpath, *Deal Management Solutions*, https://www.dealpath.com/.
3. Juniper Square, *Partnership Management Software*, https://www.junipersquare.com/.
4. Crexi, *Commercial Real Estate Platform*, https://www.crexi.com/.
5. Yardi Voyager, *Property Management Software*, https://www.yardi.com/.
6. Buildium, *Real Estate Management Solutions*, https://www.buildium.com/.
7. Prophia, *Lease Analytics Platform*, https://www.prophia.com/.
8. ATOMIQ nBrain™, *Enterprise AI Solutions*, https://www.nbrain.ai/.
9. CoStar, *Commercial Real Estate Market Data*, https://www.costar.com/.
10. Reonomy, *Commercial Real Estate Intelligence*, https://www.reonomy.com/.
11. RealPage, *Portfolio Analytics*, https://www.realpage.com/.
12. Skyline AI, *AI in Real Estate Investment*, https://www.skyline.ai/.
13. Federal Reserve Economic Data (FRED), *Economic Indicators*, https://fred.stlouisfed.org/.
14. Prophia, *Commercial Real Estate Intelligence Tools*, https://www.prophia.com/.

Section 2:

Incremental Growth Assets

5

The Bricks and Mortar of Incremental Growth Assets

Building a financial fortress capable of withstanding economic storms requires more than a strong foundation and robust cornerstones. While the keystones provide structural integrity, the day-to-day resilience of your Hard Asset Empire™ comes from the **bricks and mortar**—incremental growth assets. These "bricks" are consistent, reliable income streams like dividend-paying stocks, index funds, and other passive investments, while the "mortar" represents the cohesion that integrates these assets seamlessly into your broader strategy.

Incremental growth assets may not always grab headlines like a multimillion-dollar commercial real estate acquisition, but their role is essential. They create layers of strength, adding steady cash flow and compounding value over time. When chosen wisely and integrated with precision, these assets fortify your empire, ensuring its long-term durability and growth.

Laying the Bricks: Incremental Growth Through Passive Income Streams

The bricks of your Hard Asset Empire™ are incremental investments that deliver small but reliable returns. These investments might include:

1. **Dividend-Paying Stocks**: Shares of companies that pay regular dividends, providing a predictable income stream and compounding returns when reinvested.
2. **Index Funds**: Low-cost, broad-based funds that track market performance, offering passive exposure to equities with minimal effort.
3. **Real Estate Investment Trusts (REITs)**: Publicly traded companies that own and operate income-producing real estate, exposing you to hard assets without direct ownership.
4. **Fixed-Income Instruments**: Bonds, Treasury securities, or private debt notes that provide stable interest payments over time.

These incremental assets build wealth brick by brick, creating financial insulation against economic volatility. Unlike larger, riskier ventures, they thrive on consistency, compounding modest gains into meaningful long-term returns.

Why Incremental Growth Assets Matter

1. **Cash Flow Stability**: Dividends, bond coupons, and REIT payouts ensure regular income that can cover expenses, fund new acquisitions, or be reinvested to accelerate portfolio growth.
2. **Risk Diversification**: By balancing equity-based hard assets with smaller, passive income sources, you create a cushion against market shocks.
3. **Compounding Effect**: Reinvesting dividends and interest payments allows incremental gains to snowball over time, producing exponential results.

Example:
Imagine investing $10,000 in a diversified basket of dividend-paying stocks yielding 5% annually. By reinvesting those dividends, the investment grows through compounding—adding more shares that generate additional dividends. Over 20 years, this initial investment can grow to more than $25,000, even without further contributions.

Tools to Use:

- **M1 Finance**: Automates dividend reinvestment and portfolio management.
- **Vanguard Index Funds**: Offers low-cost, diversified index fund options.
- **Seeking Alpha**: A platform for screening high-yield dividend stocks and tracking performance.

Integrating the Mortar: Cohesion and Alignment Across Your Portfolio

The mortar binds your incremental growth assets to the larger framework of your Hard Asset Empire™. Without proper integration, these smaller investments risk becoming disjointed, undermining the efficiency and strength of your portfolio.

To ensure cohesion, focus on the following steps:

1. **Define Clear Objectives**
   Every incremental asset must serve a purpose within your broader strategy. Are you using dividends to fund additional real estate acquisitions? Are index funds providing liquidity for market downturns? Align these

goals to maximize synergy across your portfolio.

2. **Automate for Consistency**
   Automating incremental investments—such as dividend reinvestment or monthly index fund contributions—eliminates emotional decision-making and creates predictable growth. Tools like **Betterment** and **Wealthfront** simplify this process, automatically balancing your portfolio and reinvesting gains.

3. **Reinvest for Growth**
   The true power of incremental assets lies in compounding. You can accelerate portfolio expansion without requiring significant capital injections by reinvesting cash flows into new opportunities.

4. **Monitor and Adjust**
   Incremental growth assets require regular oversight to maintain alignment with your long-term vision. Use platforms like **Personal Capital** or **Morningstar** to track performance, rebalance allocations, and identify areas for improvement.

Example:

An investor earning $3,000 annually in dividends could reinvest those earnings into a passive index fund or use the cash flow to cover financing costs for a new commercial property acquisition. This incremental approach allows investors to leverage small, consistent wins to build momentum toward larger goals.

War Stories From the Alliance Vault:

Brick by Brick: How I Used Incremental Gains to Recover from a Major Loss

I've always believed that the right team is the foundation of any successful investment strategy. But I learned the hard way that not every player on the team is ready for the big leagues. Early in my career, I took a chance on a few B players—good, but not great. My mindset was that with the right leadership, I could help them develop into A players. And in many cases, I did. However, the real turning point came when I secured my first true A player and built the team around them.

An A player sets the benchmark. They operate at a higher level, anticipate challenges, and execute precisely. Once you have an A player on board, the rest of the team has to rise to their level—or they won't last. I also learned that you have to actively remove the C players. If you keep them around too long, they won't just slow you down—they'll drive your A players away.

The Broker Pivot That Changed Everything

One of the most critical team decisions I ever made was around a broker. Years ago, I had a property in Detroit that I couldn't move. My first broker was struggling—no traction, buyers, or urgency. The longer it sat, the worse the optics became. I had a choice: stick with my existing broker and hope for a turnaround or take a risk and switch.

I made the switch.

The new broker came in with a fresh approach, bigger work ethic, a different network, and an aggressive strategy. Not only did they sell the property, but they sold it at a great gain in a shorter time frame and above my original asking price. The experience completely changed my perspective on broker relationships. A great broker isn't just a transaction facilitator—they're a partner. That broker and I have done abundant deals together since, set records and become market makers in the marketplace. We both operate with the same high standards, values, and a shared mission. When you partner with the right broker, great things will happen time and time again for you, your investors, and both of your businesses.

The Mortar That Held It Together: Why Small, Consistent Wins Are More Powerful Than Big Gambles

The strategy that built Alliance wasn't flashy. It wasn't about hitting home runs on every deal or making one move that changed everything overnight. It was about stacking wins—small, consistent victories that built a foundation too strong to break.

Twenty years ago, to add to our Alliance empire's general office, industrial, and retail foundation, I decided to lean into medical office properties as part of my transactional focus. At the time, no one thought they were worth the effort. They required long-term patience, deep operational understanding, and constant engagement. But I saw something others didn't—the long game. Instead of chasing big, risky plays, I focused on steady, incremental growth and demographic certainties. Baby Boomers were only going to get older.

Commercial real estate is a marathon, not a sprint. It's about building wealth, not hoping to stumble upon it. One of my biggest lessons is that lease renewals and tenant relationships are everything. The goal isn't to squeeze the last nickel out of a deal—it's to structure a deal that works for everyone. That's how you ensure longevity, high tenant retention, and future opportunities. I turned incremental growth into a powerhouse strategy by sticking to these principles. And in the process, I built something that lasts.

Navigating Market Dynamics: The Landscape of Opportunity and Risk

No financial fortress exists in isolation. Your Hard Asset Empire™ operates within a complex, interconnected ecosystem where market dynamics dictate opportunities and risks. The success of your empire hinges on understanding these forces and positioning your investments to adapt and thrive in a competitive landscape.

Market dynamics encompass the ever-changing factors influencing asset values, tenant behavior, and investment performance. These forces include macroeconomic conditions like inflation, interest rates, employment trends, and local variables such as population growth, regulatory changes, and industry-specific developments.

Case Study: Cale Street – Strategic Navigation of Market Dynamics

Cale Street, the Kuwaiti sovereign wealth fund's investment arm, exemplifies how to navigate market dynamics effectively. Cale Street mitigates risk while capitalizing on opportunities by focusing on U.S. commercial real estate debt deals in stable, high-demand markets. Their strategy highlights two critical lessons:

1. **Focus on Stability**: Investing in areas with consistent demand minimizes exposure to volatility.
2. **Follow the Data**: A data-driven approach allows investors to identify emerging trends and align investments accordingly.

For individual investors, the same principles apply. Start by analyzing local markets where you have a knowledge advantage, then expand strategically into complementary regions or asset types that align with broader macroeconomic trends.

Step 1: Identifying High-Opportunity Markets

The cornerstone of any successful investment strategy lies in selecting markets that offer growth potential and stability. In the same way a fortress is strategically positioned on high ground or near vital resources, your Hard Asset Empire™ must be built on the foundation of well-chosen markets. Identifying these high-opportunity markets requires a methodical approach, combining data-driven insights with a keen understanding of local dynamics.

Start with Macroeconomic Indicators

Understanding macroeconomic trends is crucial to identifying markets poised for growth. Analyzing population dynamics, employment statistics, and infrastructure investments provides a broad picture of where demand is heading. Key indicators include:

- **Population Growth:** Rapid population growth is a telltale sign of rising demand for housing, retail spaces, and other hard assets. Cities like Austin, Texas, and Charlotte, North Carolina, have seen substantial growth, driven by both domestic migration and economic opportunities.
- **Job Creation and Economic Development:** Markets with a robust and diversified job market attract residents and businesses, supporting higher occupancy rates and rental growth. For example, cities

investing in technology hubs or healthcare industries often experience sustained demand across asset classes.

- **Infrastructure Expansion:** Regions that prioritize infrastructure improvements, such as new transportation corridors, utility upgrades, or technology parks, signal long-term potential. Such investments often lead to increased accessibility and a surge in property values.

Delve Into Local Market Nuances

While macro trends guide you to regions worth exploring, local market nuances are where opportunities are uncovered. It's essential to understand factors like:

- **Regulatory Environment:** Markets with landlord-friendly laws, streamlined permitting processes, and supportive local governments are more conducive to real estate investments.
- **Demographics and Consumer Behavior:** The needs and preferences of the local population, from young professionals seeking modern amenities to retirees looking for affordable and accessible living, influence asset selection.

- **Market Saturation:** Even in high-growth areas, understanding supply dynamics is critical. Overbuilt markets may face longer lease-up periods or declining rents.

For instance, analyzing Dallas–Fort Worth's booming multifamily sector, you might find that Fort Worth offers less saturated opportunities than central Dallas. By focusing on submarkets within Fort Worth that benefit from the region's overall growth, you can secure higher returns while avoiding overexposure in oversupplied areas.

Leverage Data Tools for Market Insights

Modern technology provides unparalleled access to market data, empowering investors to make informed decisions. Utilizing the right tools ensures you're basing your strategy on actionable intelligence, not guesswork.

- **CoStar:** This platform offers comprehensive market analysis, tracking trends in vacancy rates, rent growth, and new developments. For example, CoStar can help you pinpoint a submarket within a growing metro area with strong fundamentals and limited competition.

- **Reonomy:** Focused on property-level data, Reonomy provides detailed insights into ownership, historical sales, and zoning, enabling you to identify opportunities aligned with your investment criteria.
- **FRED (Federal Reserve Economic Data):** As a resource for tracking broader economic indicators like GDP growth, employment rates, and inflation trends, FRED helps investors gauge the overall health of potential markets.

These tools save time and reduce the risk of making decisions based on incomplete or outdated information.

Practical Example: Dallas–Fort Worth

Imagine an investor evaluating the Dallas–Fort Worth market. A closer look reveals that Fort Worth benefits from significant population growth, corporate relocations, and infrastructure investments. However, central Dallas is already experiencing high competition and inflated property values.

Using CoStar, the investor identifies that Fort Worth's rental demand is outpacing supply, particularly in Class B multifamily housing. Reonomy highlights properties in emerging neighborhoods with long-term value potential, and

FRED data confirms a robust economic outlook for the region. Armed with this actionable intelligence, the investor targets an underdeveloped area within Fort Worth, acquiring properties before the market becomes saturated.

This strategic approach positions the portfolio to benefit from rising rents and strong occupancy rates while mitigating risks associated with overpaying in a competitive market.

Refining Your Approach

Identifying high-opportunity markets isn't a one-time activity—it's an ongoing process. Markets evolve as conditions change, and staying ahead requires a commitment to continuous learning and adaptability.

Establish Key Performance Indicators (KPIs):

Track your target markets' rent growth, occupancy rates, and job creation. Define thresholds for what constitutes an "opportunity" and ensure every potential investment aligns with these benchmarks.

Build a Network of Local Experts:

Brokers, property managers, and developers with on-the-ground experience are invaluable resources. They provide insights that data platforms can't, such as upcoming zoning changes or shifts in tenant preferences.

Monitor Competitive Landscapes:

Use tools like CoStar to track new developments and competitor activity. Understanding the supply pipeline helps you anticipate challenges and opportunities in your target market.

Stay Informed on Policy Changes:

Local and national policies can significantly impact market dynamics. For example, changes in tax incentives or zoning laws can either open doors or create obstacles for investors.

Additional Tools to Explore

In addition to CoStar, Reonomy, and FRED, consider integrating the following tools into your market analysis strategy:

- **Local Market Reports:** Organizations like Marcus & Millichap and CBRE regularly publish market-specific reports that offer insights into regional trends and forecasts.
- **Zillow Research:** For residential investors, Zillow provides detailed market statistics, from median rents to housing inventory trends.
- **Urban Land Institute (ULI):** ULI offers in-depth studies on emerging trends, providing forward-looking perspectives on market opportunities.

Selecting high-opportunity markets is not merely about following the crowd—it's about using data and insights to uncover undervalued opportunities with strong growth potential. By combining macroeconomic analysis with local market intelligence, leveraging advanced tools, and continually refining your strategy, you position your Hard Asset Empire™ to thrive in any economic environment.

Understanding market dynamics allows you to adapt your fortress to changing conditions, ensuring that your investments are stable and primed for growth. Whether investing in a bustling metropolitan hub or a growing secondary market, the key is approaching every decision with clarity, precision, and a long-term vision. With the right tools and strategies, you can identify markets offering the best opportunities to build enduring wealth.

Step 2: Starting with Familiar Terrain

For new investors, operating in familiar markets offers a critical advantage. These markets serve as the foundation upon which you develop your investment acumen, test strategies, and build a reputation within a trusted network. Like starting construction on stable ground, beginning in a market you know well minimizes unnecessary risk while maximizing your potential for early wins.

Why Familiarity Matters

Familiarity with a market is like having a detailed blueprint—it allows you to anticipate challenges, recognize opportunities, and navigate complexities with confidence. Understanding the nuances of your local area—tenant preferences, regulatory requirements, and economic trends—gives you a distinct edge over external investors who lack this insight.

Here's how familiarity offers tangible advantages:

- **Reduced Risk Through Local Knowledge:** Knowing the intricacies of your market enables you to evaluate properties with a critical eye. You can identify undervalued opportunities, anticipate tenant behavior, and assess the impact of local events or developments.

- **Quick Response to Changes:** Familiarity allows you to stay ahead of market shifts, such as zoning law updates or shifts in tenant demographics. For instance, if a local factory closes or a new school is built, you can adjust your strategy faster than out-of-town investors.

- **Leverage Existing Relationships:** Local brokers, contractors, and property managers already in your network can provide access to off-market deals, insights into neighborhood trends, and reliable support for property management and renovations.

- **Enhanced Credibility:** Building a local reputation as a knowledgeable and trustworthy investor fosters referrals and collaboration. Brokers are more likely to prioritize you when presenting new deals, and local tenants may feel more confident renting from someone embedded in the community.

Practical Example: Chicago Multifamily Investments

Let's consider a Chicago-based investor looking to get started in real estate. Familiarity with the city's unique neighborhoods, tenant preferences, and redevelopment trends gives them a strong foundation. For example, they may notice early signs of gentrification in a historically working-class neighborhood: new cafes and boutiques, increased public transit investments, and rising property sales.

With this knowledge, the investor focuses on acquiring small multifamily properties in these areas. Their local expertise allows them to:

- Understand tenant demographics, ensuring the properties meet demand for amenities like bike storage or shared workspaces.
- Avoid overpaying for properties by assessing comparable sales with a nuanced understanding.
- Secure reliable contractors and property managers already operating in the neighborhood.

This local focus reduces risk and positions the investor to benefit from long-term appreciation and consistent rental income.

The Role of Relationships in Familiar Markets

Local relationships are one of the greatest assets for an investor starting in familiar terrain. These connections provide access to off-market opportunities, professional support, and real-time market updates.

- **Brokers and Bird Dogs:** Trusted brokers and bird dogs (deal scouts) can alert you to high-value opportunities before they hit public listings. Developing a track record with local brokers ensures they see you as a reliable buyer.

- **Contractors and Property Managers:** Working with local professionals reduces logistical challenges and ensures your projects are handled by experienced individuals familiar with the area's regulations and expectations.

- **Community Leaders and Officials:** Engaging with city planners, zoning officials, and local business leaders provides insights into upcoming development projects and regulatory changes. For example, a conversation with a city official might reveal that a particular area is slated for new public transit infrastructure, signaling potential growth.

Leveraging Tools for Local Market Success

While relationships and intuition play a significant role, technology enhances your ability to analyze and act within familiar markets. Combining your local knowledge with powerful tools gives you a comprehensive understanding of your target area.

- **Local Government Websites:** Many city and county websites provide access to zoning maps, economic development plans, and demographic data. For instance, Chicago's Department of Planning and Development offers detailed insights into neighborhood revitalization projects.

- **Broker Networks and Platforms:** Platforms like Crexi and CoStar allow you to explore commercial listings, analyze market trends, and connect with brokers specializing in your area.

- **Community Data Tools:** Resources like Zillow Research or Redfin Market Trends can provide neighborhood-level housing prices, rental demand, and inventory data.

Expanding in Familiar Terrain: A Systematic Approach

Operating in a familiar market doesn't mean staying static—it means starting with what you know and systematically building on that foundation. Here's a step-by-step guide:

1. **Conduct a Micro-Market Analysis:** Go beyond city-wide statistics to analyze specific neighborhoods or districts. Identify areas with favorable trends like rising rental demand, declining vacancy rates, or significant infrastructure investments.

2. **Build a Trusted Network:** Deepen your relationships with brokers, contractors, and property managers. Attend local real estate meetups or join city-based

investor groups to expand your connections.

3. **Test Strategies on a Smaller Scale:** Use your first investments as learning experiences. For instance, purchase a duplex or triplex in a neighborhood you understand well, and focus on optimizing operations and tenant satisfaction before scaling up.

4. **Track Performance:** Monitor the performance of your initial investments to refine your approach. Use tools like Stessa to track income, expenses, and ROI.

5. **Leverage Referrals:** As you establish yourself locally, leverage referrals from tenants, brokers, and other stakeholders to uncover additional opportunities.

Scaling Outward While Staying Grounded

Once you've built a strong foundation in your local market, consider using it as a launchpad for scaling outward. Expanding into adjacent neighborhoods, similar property types, or nearby cities allows you to leverage your existing knowledge while diversifying your portfolio.

For example, an investor who has successfully acquired and managed multifamily properties in Chicago might expand into nearby markets like Milwaukee or Indianapolis. These cities share demographic and economic similarities but offer unique growth opportunities.

Case Study: The Power of Familiar Terrain

Imagine an investor in Austin, Texas, who initially focused on acquiring single-family rental properties in South Austin, an area they know intimately. Over time, they develop relationships with local contractors, property managers, and brokers. Their deep understanding of tenant preferences—like proximity to tech hubs and access to outdoor spaces—allows them to secure long-term tenants and maintain high occupancy rates.

With this experience, they pivot to small multifamily properties in similar neighborhoods, leveraging their knowledge of local market trends and scaling their portfolio without overextending. When they consider expanding to other cities like San Antonio or Dallas, they have a proven track record, a scalable strategy, and a network of trusted contacts.

Starting with familiar terrain is not just a safe entry point—it's a strategic advantage. By leveraging local knowledge, building strong relationships, and using targeted tools, you can minimize risk, uncover unique opportunities, and establish a solid foundation for your Hard Asset Empire™. Familiarity provides the confidence and credibility needed to execute successful investments while building the expertise to expand into new markets.

With each successful deal, you'll sharpen your skills, strengthen your network, and prepare for the next phase of your journey: scaling beyond familiar markets while maintaining the stability and integrity of your financial fortress. By starting where you know best, you set yourself up for a future of informed, sustainable growth.

Step 3: Expanding to Complementary Markets

Once your foothold in a familiar market is secure, the natural progression is to expand into complementary markets that align with your portfolio's strengths and long-term strategy. This stage is akin to adding extensions to your financial fortress, carefully selecting new territories that enhance and reinforce the overall structure. Complementary markets often share characteristics with your existing investments, such as similar demographics, economic conditions, or tenant profiles, but offer opportunities for diversification and growth.

Identifying Complementary Markets

Complementary markets either build on your existing expertise or allow you to leverage established relationships and systems. The goal is to expand without overextending by targeting markets with dynamics you already understand.

For example:

- **Shared Demographics:** If your portfolio includes multifamily properties catering to young professionals, expanding into a market with a similar demographic profile—such as a city experiencing a tech boom—can provide a smooth transition.
- **Economic Conditions:** Markets with steady job growth, low unemployment, and robust infrastructure investments create fertile ground for new opportunities.
- **Tenant Preferences:** If you have experience working with logistics tenants in industrial spaces, expanding into markets near major ports or transportation hubs aligns with your existing expertise.

The Role of Sector Trends

Sector-specific trends often dictate which markets to enter next. Expanding into complementary markets requires understanding the drivers of growth in your chosen asset class:

1. **E-Commerce and Industrial Spaces:**
   The rapid growth of online shopping continues to drive demand for warehouses, fulfillment centers, and logistics hubs. Areas near major transportation networks—such as Los Angeles or Dallas—are prime targets for industrial investments.

2. **Aging Populations and Medical Office Buildings:**
   An aging demographic creates a consistent need for healthcare services. Cities with high senior populations, like Phoenix or Sarasota, are ideal locations for medical office investments.

3. **Urbanization and Multifamily Housing:**
   Urban centers experiencing population growth often sustain strong demand for rental housing. Targeting cities with expanding job markets and rising rental rates ensures consistent cash flow and long-term appreciation.

Practical Example: Diversifying Beyond Multifamily

An investor with a successful track record in the Midwest multifamily market might consider expanding into industrial assets in Southern California. Proximity to ports like Long Beach and Los Angeles drives demand for warehouse and logistics facilities. By leveraging their experience in property management and tenant relations, the investor can diversify their portfolio while capitalizing on a booming sector.

Tools to Leverage

Effective expansion requires tools that provide actionable insights and help identify underperforming sectors or untapped opportunities:

- **Prophia:** Analyze lease data and market trends to determine which sectors and regions offer the most potential.
- **RealPage Analytics:** Evaluate tenant preferences, market dynamics, and competitive benchmarks.
- **CoStar:** Access comprehensive market intelligence to identify high-growth regions and forecast trends.

Establishing a Stronghold in New Markets

As you expand, focus on replicating the systems and strategies that brought success in your core market.

Standardized processes for acquisitions, property management, and tenant relations streamline the transition to new territories. Additionally, maintain flexibility to adapt to the unique characteristics of each new market.

Step 4: Adapting to Shifts in Market Dynamics

Building a Hard Asset Empire™ isn't a static endeavor—it requires constant vigilance and adaptability. Market dynamics evolve due to economic disruptions, technological advancements, and regulatory changes, and your financial fortress must evolve alongside them. Adapting to these shifts ensures that your portfolio remains resilient and profitable, even as the world around it changes.

Navigating Economic Disruptions

Economic fluctuations are inevitable, but investors who prepare for these challenges gain a competitive edge. By focusing on recession-proof assets and strategic debt management, you can protect your portfolio from volatility and position it for growth during recovery periods.

1. **Recession-Proof Assets:**
   Asset classes like affordable multifamily housing, medical office buildings, and industrial spaces tend to

remain stable during downturns. These investments provide consistent cash flow, even in challenging economic conditions.

2. **Interest Rate Volatility:**
   Rising interest rates can increase borrowing costs and compress margins. Lock in favorable debt terms during periods of low interest rates or explore alternative financing options, such as adjustable-rate loans with caps or private equity partnerships, to hedge against rate hikes

Embracing Technological Advancements

Technology is reshaping every aspect of the real estate industry, from property management to investment analysis. Embracing these advancements allows you to operate more efficiently, attract tenants, and identify emerging opportunities.

1. **Smart Buildings and Standards:**
   Energy-efficient technology, such as smart thermostats and solar panels, reduces operating costs while meeting the growing demand for environmentally sustainable properties. Tenants increasingly favor buildings that align with energy efficient principles, providing a competitive

advantage.

2. **AI-Driven Insights:**
   Again this is where you leverage your tools like Retrieval-Augmented Generation (RAG) AI models to synthesize vast amounts of market data, predict trends, and recommend tailored strategies. For example, AI can identify underperforming assets in your portfolio and suggest value-add opportunities, such as renovations or lease renegotiations.

Practical Example: Pivoting During the COVID-19 Pandemic

The COVID-19 pandemic disrupted traditional office markets as remote work became the norm. Investors who anticipated this shift and pivoted to flexible coworking spaces or suburban office parks with outdoor amenities saw continued demand while traditional office spaces struggled. By embracing technology and adapting to tenant needs, these investors preserved cash flow and positioned their portfolios for long-term success.

Case Study: Riding the Industrial Boom

The rise of e-commerce presents a compelling example of adapting to market dynamics. One investor recognized the growing demand for industrial spaces and targeted regions near major transportation hubs, such as Reno, Nevada, and Dallas, Texas. Leveraging tools like CoStar for market analysis and Yardi Voyager for tenant insights, they acquired properties with low vacancy rates and high tenant demand.

The investor achieved consistent NOI growth and stable cash flow by focusing on high-growth regions and negotiating long-term leases with e-commerce tenants. Additionally, incorporating smart building technology reduced operating expenses, further boosting profitability.

Practical Steps for Staying Ahead

1. **Monitor Leading Indicators:**
   Use tools like Federal Reserve Economic Data (FRED) to track economic trends such as GDP growth, employment rates, and consumer spending.

2. **Engage With Emerging Trends:**
   Stay informed about technological advancements,

such as AI-driven asset management platforms and renewable energy solutions, to maintain a competitive edge.

3. **Develop Contingency Plans:**
   Regularly stress-test your portfolio against potential scenarios, such as economic downturns or regulatory changes, to identify vulnerabilities and develop proactive solutions.

4. **Maintain Liquidity:**
   Having liquid reserves allows you to capitalize on opportunities during market disruptions, such as acquiring distressed assets at favorable prices.

Thriving Amid Change

Adapting to market dynamics is an ongoing process that requires vigilance, flexibility, and a willingness to embrace change. By staying attuned to economic shifts, leveraging technology, and focusing on resilient asset classes, you can build a portfolio that survives and thrives in any environment.

The **Hard Asset Empire Blueprint™** equips you with the tools and strategies to navigate uncertainty with confidence. Expanding into complementary markets and adapting to changes proactively creates a financial fortress designed to endure. In the next chapter, we'll delve deeper into incremental growth assets—the bricks and mortar that add layers of strength and durability to your empire.

Step 5: Aligning with Global Trends

As your **Hard Asset Empire™** evolves, aligning your strategy with global economic and geopolitical trends becomes increasingly important. These larger forces create waves that can either propel your investments forward or sweep them into turbulent waters. While local market knowledge provides a foundation, understanding global trends ensures your portfolio remains relevant and resilient in a rapidly changing world.

The Role of Global Trends

Global trends influence asset values, financing options, and tenant preferences. By staying ahead of these shifts, you position yourself to capitalize on emerging opportunities while mitigating risks. Some of the most significant global trends shaping market dynamics include:

1. **Decentralized Finance (DeFi) and Blockchain Technology**
   Blockchain technology and decentralized finance are transforming the real estate industry. From tokenized assets to smart contracts, these innovations reduce transaction costs, increase transparency, and democratize investment access. For example, real estate tokenization allows investors to purchase fractional ownership in high-value properties, broadening the pool of potential buyers and enhancing liquidity.

   Practical Example:
   A commercial real estate investor could leverage DeFi platforms to tokenize the future or existing cash flows and value of their property and raise funds for a project, bypassing traditional financing routes and tapping into a growing community of global crypto investors who want to diversify into hard assets like real estate through tokenized ownership.

2. **Urban-to-Suburban Migration**
   The pandemic accelerated a shift in housing demand

as remote work enabled many to leave urban centers for suburban and secondary markets. This trend has created opportunities in areas with affordable housing, good schools, and access to outdoor spaces. Suburban multifamily properties and single-family rental homes are becoming increasingly attractive asset classes.

Practical Example:
An investor recognizing this trend might pivot from urban high-rise developments to suburban rental properties, focusing on regions like Austin, Texas, or Charlotte, North Carolina, where population growth and job creation intersect.

3. **Foreign Investment and Capital Flows**
   Monitoring international capital flows can provide valuable insights into emerging markets. Investors from regions with unstable currencies or political uncertainty often seek safe havens for their wealth, driving demand in stable markets. Tracking these flows helps identify areas where increased competition and rising property values are likely.

Practical Example:
An influx of foreign investment into U.S. industrial properties signals strong confidence in the sector. By entering these markets early, an investor can secure prime assets before competition intensifies.

Tools to Leverage

Understanding global trends requires access to reliable, up-to-date information. The following tools provide the data and analysis necessary to align your strategy with broader economic forces:

1. **Alliance Intelligence Newsletter**
   This curated resource offers insights into macroeconomic trends, geopolitical developments, and market forecasts, helping investors stay ahead of the curve. https://www.subscribetoben.com

2. **Bloomberg Terminal**
   A premier platform for global market data, the Bloomberg Terminal provides in-depth analysis of capital flows, economic indicators, and industry-specific trends.

3. **CoStar Group**
   CoStar's market intelligence tools allow you to assess

how global trends are impacting local markets, providing a bridge between macro and microanalysis.

4. **ATOMIQ nBrain™**
   https://www.nbrain.tech This open source enterprise AI agent (RAG model) platform can be customized to integrate global and local data sources, synthesizing insights to guide decision-making. Whether predicting tenant demand shifts or evaluating regulatory changes' impact, nBrain™ ensures you remain agile and informed.

Practical Steps for Aligning With Global Trends

1. **Track Economic Indicators:**
   Monitor GDP growth, inflation rates, and currency stability in key regions to anticipate shifts in demand and financing conditions.

2. **Adopt Emerging Technologies:**
   Explore blockchain platforms for asset tokenization and consider integrating smart contracts to streamline transactions and reduce costs.

3. **Engage With International Stakeholders:**
   Build relationships with foreign investors, developers,

and lenders to gain access to global capital and expertise.

4. **Diversify Across Markets:**
   Hedge against local downturns by expanding into international or cross-border markets with favorable demographic and economic conditions.

Case Study: Capitalizing on Suburban Growth

A real estate investment firm noticed the pandemic-driven migration to suburban markets and identified Phoenix, Arizona, as a high-opportunity area. Using tools like Prophia for lease analytics and CoStar for demographic insights, the firm acquired a portfolio of suburban multifamily properties. By aligning their strategy with the urban-to-suburban migration trend, they achieved high occupancy rates and rental growth, significantly enhancing their NOI.

Navigating market dynamics is both an art and a science. By aligning your strategy with global trends, you expand your perspective beyond local markets and gain the ability to anticipate shifts that impact your portfolio. Whether leveraging blockchain for decentralized financing, capitalizing on suburban migration patterns, or monitoring foreign investment flows, staying attuned to these trends ensures that your **Hard Asset Empire™** remains adaptive and resilient.

Investors who embrace tools like the **Alliance Intelligence Newsletter, Bloomberg Terminal, CoStar Group**, and **ATOMIQ's nBrain™** gain a competitive edge. These resources provide actionable insights that empower you to identify opportunities, mitigate risks, and refine your strategy.

Building a successful **Hard Asset Empire™** requires vigilance, adaptability, and a willingness to explore new frontiers. By starting in familiar terrain, expanding into complementary markets, adapting to shifting dynamics, and aligning with global trends, you create a portfolio that not only withstands economic turbulence but thrives in it.

Key Takeaways

- **Start Local:** Begin with markets you understand, leveraging local knowledge to reduce risk and build credibility.
- **Expand Strategically:** Enter complementary markets that align with your portfolio's strengths and long-term objectives.

- **Adapt Proactively:** Anticipate and respond to market shifts, using data and technology to stay ahead of the curve.
- **Think Globally:** Align your strategy with global trends to capitalize on emerging opportunities and diversify risk.

Your **Hard Asset Empire™** doesn't just exist in isolation; it operates within a dynamic, interconnected landscape. By mastering market dynamics and staying attuned to local and global forces, you ensure that your financial fortress stands strong against the winds of change, ready to seize the opportunities.

The Bricks, The Mortar, and the Future

Incremental growth assets are not flashy, but they are indispensable. They form the bricks that build layers of financial strength and the mortar that holds your portfolio together, integrating small wins into a cohesive and resilient system. Whether through dividend-paying stocks, index funds, or REITs, these investments provide the stability and compounding growth needed to weather economic storms and take advantage of future opportunities.

By methodically adding these incremental layers of income and reinvesting gains, you create a self-sustaining engine for growth. Coupled with a deep understanding of market dynamics and a data-driven approach, your Hard Asset Empire™ gains the durability and momentum needed to thrive for generations.

In the next chapter, we'll explore **The Steel Framing: Resilience Mechanisms,** where asset protection strategies, insurance, and tax planning provide the structural integrity that defends your financial fortress against external pressures and unforeseen challenges.

Endnotes

1. CoStar Group, *Market Analysis and Trends*, https://www.costar.com/.
2. Reonomy, *Commercial Real Estate Intelligence*, https://www.reonomy.com/.
3. Federal Reserve Economic Data (FRED), *Economic Indicators*, https://fred.stlouisfed.org/.
4. Prophia, *Lease and Market Analytics*, https://www.prophia.com/.
5. RealPage, *Portfolio and Tenant Analytics*, https://www.realpage.com/.
6. nBrain™, *RAG Model AI Platform for Asset Management and Decision Making*, https://nbrain.tech/.
7. Yardi Voyager, *Comprehensive Property Management Software*, https://www.yardi.com/.
8. Buildium, *Property Management for Multifamily and Single-Family Assets*, https://www.buildium.com/.
9. Crexi, *Commercial Real Estate Listings and Market Insights*, https://www.crexi.com/.
10. Alliance Intelligence Newsletter, *Market Trends and Resilience Strategies*, https://subscribetoben.com/.
11. Bloomberg Terminal, *Global Market Data and Analysis*, https://www.bloomberg.com/professional/.
12. RealPage Portfolio Analytics, *Optimize Portfolio Performance*, https://www.realpage.com/.
13. Marcus & Millichap, *2024 Commercial Real Estate Trends Report*, https://www.marcusmillichap.com/.
14. Deloitte, *Real Estate Predictions 2024*, https://www2.deloitte.com/.
15. Urban Land Institute, *Emerging Trends in Real Estate 2024*, https://uli.org/.
16. Stessa, *Rental Property Financial Management*, https://www.stessa.com/.
17. Altus Group, *Scenario Analysis for Real Estate*, https://www.altusgroup.com/.
18. Juniper Square, *Investor and Equity Partnership Management*, https://www.junipersquare.com/.
19. Crexi, *Broker and Deal Sourcing Platform*, https://www.crexi.com/.
20. Buildium, *Tenant and Lease Management Software*, https://www.buildium.com/.
21. Prophia, *AI-Driven Lease Analytics*, https://www.prophia.com/.
22. Yardi Breeze, *Expense Tracking for Real Estate*, https://www.yardibreeze.com/.
23. Skyline AI, *AI in Real Estate Investment*, https://www.skyline.ai/.

24. Tableau, *Data Visualization for Real Estate*, https://www.tableau.com/.
25. Crowdstreet, *Fundamentals of CRE Investing*, https://www.crowdstreet.com/.
26. JP Morgan Private Bank, *Commercial Real Estate Outlook*, https://privatebank.jpmorgan.com/.
27. LUMI Commercial Real Estate, *Asset Protection for Commercial Real Estate*, https://lumicre.com/.
28. Dominion, *Asset Protection for Real Estate Investors*, https://www.dominion.com/.
29. Stratafolio, *How to Protect Your Commercial Real Estate Assets*, https://stratafolio.com/.
30. Huguelet Law, *4 Levels of Asset Protection for Real Estate Investors*, https://www.hugueletlaw.com/.

6

Resilient Wealth with Steel-Strong Reinforcements

No fortress can stand without structural integrity. While bricks, mortar, and foundations give your Hard Asset Empire™ strength, the steel framing provides resilience—the ability to withstand the unexpected. Resilience mechanisms such as insurance, asset protection, and tax planning are the framework that shields your financial fortress from external pressures, economic shocks, and personal challenges. As steel girders ensure that buildings remain intact during earthquakes and storms, these mechanisms prevent your empire from crumbling when adversity strikes.

Building wealth is not just about accumulation; it's about protection. It's about preparing for the worst while positioning yourself for the best. This chapter will guide you step by step through the strategies, tools, and mindsets required to implement a comprehensive resilience plan. We'll explore how to shield your assets, minimize tax liabilities, and ensure your fortress remains unshaken, no matter your challenges. It is "inside the walls" of your empire where you must embed resilience mechanisms and secure vaults for everything from your personal, portfolio, business, and family's operational security (OpSec), but also your cybersecurity and data privacy protections, and succession plans. This chapter will walk you through what you need to do to embed resilience into your **Hard Asset Empire Blueprint™**.

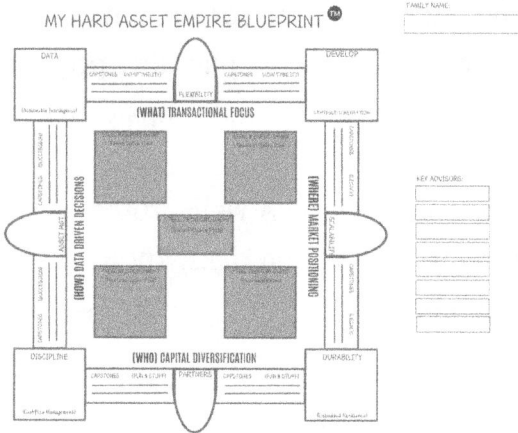

MY HARD ASSET EMPIRE BLUEPRINT™

The Role of Embedded Resilience in Wealth-Building

Resilience in wealth-building isn't reactive—it's proactive or embedded by design. Waiting until a crisis strikes to think about asset protection, insurance, or tax strategy is like attempting to reinforce a building mid-earthquake. The true strength of resilience lies in preparing for challenges long before they appear.

Resilience mechanisms achieve three critical goals:

1. Mitigating Risks: Insurance and asset protection strategies reduce financial exposure during lawsuits, accidents, or economic downturns.
2. Ensuring Stability: Tax planning preserves cash flow, minimizes liabilities, and keeps your empire's resources intact.
3. Creating Flexibility: A well-protected structure allows you to take calculated risks, knowing you have safety nets in place.

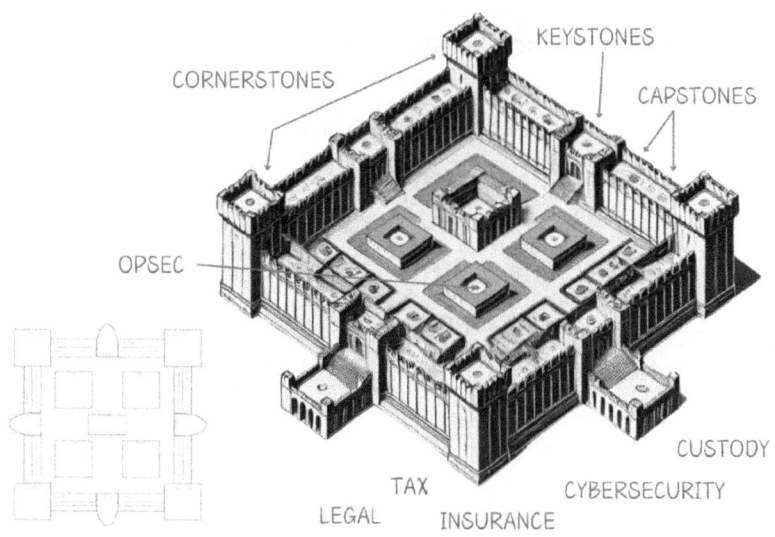

HARD ASSET EMPIRE BLUEPRINT™

KEYSTONES

CORNERSTONES

CAPSTONES

OPSEC

CUSTODY

TAX

CYBERSECURITY

LEGAL

INSURANCE

Insurance – The Steel Safety Net for Your Financial Fortress

Insurance is more than a checkbox in your financial plan—the steel safety net covers your Hard Asset Empire™ against unforeseen calamities. While it's easy to view insurance as a necessary expense, seeing it as a strategic investment in resilience is more productive. Properly structured insurance policies can protect your hard assets, income streams, and long-term plans from disruptions that might otherwise derail your wealth-building journey.

The Role of Insurance in Wealth Preservation

Insurance is a safety net, ensuring your portfolio can withstand shocks and grow even under adverse circumstances. Whether it's a natural disaster damaging a key property, a liability lawsuit threatening your cash flow, or losing a critical team member; insurance provides the financial buffer needed to recover and move forward without sacrificing long-term goals.

Essential Types of Insurance for Your Empire

1. Property Insurance: Safeguarding Tangible Assets

Property insurance is the backbone of any real estate portfolio's risk management strategy. It covers damages caused by fires, floods, theft, or vandalism. Each asset class—multifamily housing, industrial warehouses, or medical office buildings—has unique risk factors, and policies should be tailored accordingly.

- **For multifamily housing:** Policies should cover tenant-related damages, maintenance delays, and infrastructure issues.
- **For industrial properties:** Focus on risks related to heavy equipment, high-value inventories, and logistics.
- **For office buildings:** Include coverage for tenant improvements and business continuity.

Pro Tip: Ensure your policies account for replacement costs rather than just market value. The cost of rebuilding is often higher than the depreciated value of the asset.

---

2. Liability Insurance: Protecting Against Legal Fallout

Liability lawsuits can arise from tenant injuries, negligence claims, or even environmental hazards on your property. A robust commercial general liability (CGL) policy shields you from financial loss by covering legal fees, settlements, and judgments.

- **Examples of risks covered:**
  - A tenant slips on icy stairs in your multifamily property.
  - A client is injured while visiting your office building.
  - A warehouse fire causes damages that disrupt neighboring businesses.

Pro Tip: Partner liability clauses in lease agreements can reduce exposure by sharing the responsibility for accidents with tenants or contractors.

---

3. Umbrella Insurance: The Ultimate Backstop

Umbrella insurance acts as an additional layer of protection that kicks in when your primary liability coverage is exhausted. In today's litigious environment, a single major lawsuit can exceed standard policy limits, making umbrella coverage indispensable.

- **Scenario:** If a multifamily tenant sues for negligence after a fire and wins a $3 million judgment, your CGL policy may cover only $1 million. An umbrella policy fills the $2 million gap.

4. Key-Person Life Insurance: Securing Continuity

Key-person insurance is vital if you run a real estate business or have partners who play pivotal roles in decision-making and operations. This policy compensates for the financial impact of losing a critical team member, ensuring the company can continue while a replacement is found or operations are restructured.

- **Practical Example:** A real estate fund loses its founding partner, integral to sourcing deals and securing financing. Key-person insurance provides the liquidity needed to keep the firm afloat during the transition.

---

5. Business Interruption Insurance: Preserving Cash Flow

When disaster strikes, such as a hurricane or fire that temporarily renders a property unusable, business interruption insurance ensures you can continue meeting financial obligations like mortgage payments, payroll, and operating expenses.

- **How it works:** If an industrial warehouse is damaged in a storm, this coverage replaces lost rental income until the property is operational.

Pro Tip: Pair business interruption insurance with disaster recovery plans to reduce downtime.

Practical Steps for Implementing an Insurance Plan

1. Conduct a Comprehensive Risk Audit

Start by identifying vulnerabilities in your portfolio. Consider factors such as geographic location, tenant demographics, and property-specific risks. For example:

- **Geography:** Properties in hurricane-prone areas may require flood insurance.
- **Tenant Risks:** Multifamily properties with higher turnover may face more frequent liability claims.

2. Partner With a Specialist Broker

A broker who specializes in commercial real estate insurance can tailor policies to your needs. They'll also keep you informed about changes in regulations or coverage options. For example:

- Brokers at Hub International specialize in crafting policies for real estate investors, ensuring coverage is aligned with your strategic objectives.

3. Layer Your Coverage

A layered approach combines property insurance, liability policies, and umbrella coverage to create a comprehensive safety net. This redundancy ensures no single event can jeopardize your financial position.

4. Regularly Review and Update Policies

As your portfolio grows and market conditions evolve, revisit your insurance plan. An annual review ensures your coverage keeps pace with new acquisitions, increasing property values, or emerging risks.

5. Leverage Technology for Risk Management

Modern tools can help you assess vulnerabilities and track your coverage more effectively:

- **Riskalyze:** Evaluate risk exposure across your portfolio.
- **Procore:** Tracks property conditions to reduce maintenance-related claims.

War Stories from the Alliance Vault:

The Shield That Saved Me: How Asset Protection Stopped a Lawsuit From Destroying My Future

One of the smartest moves I ever made wasn't a real estate deal—it was the decision to map out a master plan for estate and asset protection. I wasn't just building a business; I was structuring my entire life to ensure long-term security. I sat down with an expert and ensured every detail was covered and I encourage you to do the same.

SIDENOTE: The person who recommended or maybe even gave you this book may have been one of my Alliance ecosystem partners and Hard Asset Empire™ Ambassadors or advisors. Surround yourself with people who can help you properly structure these embedded reinforcements for asset protection and ensure you invest the time and money required to protect your *assets.*

When I came away from that meeting with my experts, I was empowered by asking these three (3) critical questions:

- *What entities/assets should hold risk?*
- *Which entities/assets should capture the gain?*

- *How could I effectively operate while keeping a protective shield around my family and future?*

This planning made me a ghost in the right ways—visible where needed, but legally structured to prevent unnecessary exposure. It ensured that no single lawsuit, investment mishap, or market downturn could dismantle everything I had built.

Protecting Myself Through Refinances

Real estate isn't just about buying and selling; it's about structuring financial resilience. Every refinance I do is designed to protect both my personal risk and the interests of my investors.

A perfect example is the Largo, Florida, deal. Several years into the asset, we lost our tenant and the property was vacant when the current loan came due and we were in default. The problem was that the value of the investment had dropped below the debt owed. This left us with only a few options and the lender didn't want to extend the loan. The loan was a 50% limited guaranty recourse loan, but because I was worth nothing on paper, my financial and asset protection structure became a key leverage point. Because of how I had set things up with my asset protection strategy, the lender realized they had no choice but to work it out with me—they couldn't force an outcome that wasn't in my favor. My structure made me indispensable in the deal, leading to a win-win resolution in the workout as we decided to sell the property via auction and produced a successful outcome for all parties. It was a validating lesson regarding personal asset protection and corporate financial structure. It was also a reminder that the only reason someone has you "guarantee" the loan is to keep you vested in the process.

Feature	Recourse Loan	Non-Recourse Loan
Lender's Rights	Pursue borrower's personal assets	Limited to collateral only
Borrower Risk	Higher	Lower
Lender Risk	Lower	Higher
Interest Rates	Lower	Higher
Loan Types	Construction, bridge loans	Stabilized income properties
Examples	Bank loans	Fannie Mae®, Freddie Mac® loans

Another key principle I've learned: If you're not willing to offer a non-recourse deal, I'm not willing to finance my deal with you. I know the value of protecting my position, and I don't deviate from it. I walk if lenders or partners won't play by those terms or remove it when I offer to put more equity into the capital stack. Sure it may cost me a deal now and again, but I sleep better at night and there is always another deal to be made. Removing risk is as important as generating incremental return.

Lessons in Resilience

1. ***Protect Yourself Before You Need It*** – *The time to structure asset protection isn't after a lawsuit or loss; it's before one ever arises.*
2. **Surround Yourself with Outstanding Advisors** – Work out a long-term relationship with them that allows you to pay them, but with someone who wants to be a part of your long-term vision and inner circle. Key attributes are competent, dependable, reliable, trustworthy, and provide a safe space to be vulnerable.
3. ***Control Your Leverage*** – *The right financial structure can turn a lender from an adversary into a collaborator.*
4. ***Hold Firm on Non-Recourse Deals*** – *If a deal doesn't align with your risk mitigation strategy, be willing to walk away.*
5. ***Use the Tax Code Strategically*** – *Smart structuring isn't about avoidance—it's about positioning for optimal financial security.*

Resilience in real estate isn't just about having money in the bank. It's about structuring every aspect of your operation to withstand pressure, adapt to challenges, and keep moving forward—no matter what.

Recommended Tools for Implementing Insurance Strategies

1. **Hub International:** Specializes in real estate-focused insurance solutions, providing tailored coverage for diverse portfolios.
2. **The Hartford:** Offers customizable business and liability policies, ideal for landlords and property owners.
3. **Riskalyze:** A platform for evaluating portfolio risk exposure and identifying insurance gaps.
4. **Procore:** Tracks property conditions and maintenance schedules, reducing liability risks.

The Bigger Picture: Building Resilience

Insurance is just one piece of the resilience puzzle, but it's a critical one. Creating a robust safety net with property, liability, and umbrella coverage ensures that your Hard Asset Empire™ can withstand unexpected challenges and continue growing. The security provided by these policies allows you to focus on strategic expansion and seizing new opportunities, knowing that your foundation is protected.

The next section will explore additional resilience mechanisms, including asset protection strategies and tax planning, to further reinforce your financial fortress. Together, these elements form the steel frame that supports your empire through the storms of uncertainty.

Asset Protection – The Steel Shield Against Threats

While insurance protects your financial fortress against specific, external events, asset protection fortifies it against legal and financial threats, such as lawsuits, creditors, or unforeseen liabilities. These strategies are the shields bolted onto your fortress walls, ensuring your wealth remains intact and your empire resilient against breaches.

Key Asset Protection Strategies

1. **Limited Liability Companies (LLCs): The First Layer of Defense** LLCs are real estate investors' foundation of asset protection. You separate personal assets from business liabilities by holding properties within individual LLCs. This separation ensures that a legal claim or lawsuit against one property cannot threaten your entire portfolio.

Example: A tenant sues for injuries sustained due to an accident in one of your multifamily buildings. If that property is owned by an LLC, only the assets within that LLC are at risk. Your personal assets and other properties held in separate LLCs remain insulated.

Practical Recommendation:
Work with experienced attorneys to structure LLCs correctly. While platforms like LegalZoom provide basic LLC setup services, dedicated specialists like Wyoming LLC Attorney offer customized solutions tailored to real estate portfolios, including multi-layered protections for state-specific regulations.

---

2. **Series LLCs: Compartmentalizing Risk** For investors with multiple properties, Series LLCs provide a powerful mechanism for compartmentalization. A Series LLC operates like a master LLC containing individual "cells," each legally independent from the others. If one cell faces a lawsuit or financial claim, the others remain unaffected.

Why Use Series LLCs:

- o Streamlined management: Maintain a single overarching LLC while separating risks across assets.
- o Cost efficiency: Save on administrative fees compared to forming individual LLCs for each property.

3. **Example:**

An investor with 10 rental properties can place each into a separate series within a single Series LLC. A liability claim against one property, such as a tenant injury, cannot extend to the other nine.

---

3. **Trust Structures: Transferring and Protecting Wealth** Trusts are advanced asset protection tools that serve dual purposes: shielding assets from creditors and facilitating legacy planning.

- o **Revocable Living Trusts:**
  Useful for estate planning, these trusts allow you to maintain control over your assets during

your lifetime. However, they offer limited protection against lawsuits or creditors.

- ○ **Irrevocable Trusts:**
  Assets transferred into an irrevocable trust are removed from your estate, making them inaccessible to creditors or litigants. These trusts are ideal for long-term wealth preservation and family legacy planning.

4. **Example:**

   A commercial real estate investor places a $10 million property portfolio into an irrevocable trust. If a lawsuit targets the investor, the trust's assets are protected, as they are no longer legally owned by the individual.

---

4. **Equity Stripping: Reducing Attractiveness to Creditors** Equity stripping is a strategy that reduces the equity in your properties by taking on secured debt, such as a mortgage or line of credit. Minimizing equity makes your properties less appealing to creditors or litigants seeking financial compensation.

   Example:
   A $5 million office building may carry $4.8 million in secured debt, leaving only $200,000 of exposed equity. In the event of a lawsuit, the limited equity discourages creditors from pursuing claims against the asset.

   Pro Tip:
   While equity stripping can be a powerful tool for asset protection and financial flexibility, it must be executed

carefully to avoid legal disputes, financial strain, or unintended consequences. Consulting legal and financial professionals is essential when considering this strategy. Work with lenders who understand this strategy and can offer favorable financing terms. Structured correctly, equity stripping can enhance both asset protection and cash flow management.

Aspect	Rewards	Risks
Asset Protection	Shields assets from creditors	May be challenged as fraudulent conveyance
Control	Retains ownership and cash flow	Over-leveraging risks financial strain
Legal Shielding	Enhances protection when paired with LLCs	Complex legal setup and costs
Financial Access	Provides liquidity through HELOCs	Risk of negative credit impact
Creditor Deterrence	Reduces likelihood of lawsuits	Vulnerable in declining real estate markets

5. **Homestead Exemptions: Safeguarding Your Primary Residence** Many states offer legal protections for a primary residence through homestead exemptions, shielding it from creditor claims up to a certain value. While this is not directly applicable to investment properties, understanding and utilizing your state's homestead laws ensures your

personal living situation remains secure.

 Example:
A Florida investor's primary residence worth $500,000 is fully protected under the state's generous homestead exemption, even if creditors pursue other personal assets.

Practical Steps to Implement Asset Protection

1. **Structure Your Holdings** Move each real estate asset into its own LLC or Series LLC. This compartmentalization ensures that a single lawsuit or claim cannot jeopardize your entire portfolio.

2. **Partner With Legal Experts** Asset protection is complex and requires state-specific strategies. Partner with attorneys specializing in real estate and asset protection law, such as LLC Attorney, for guidance on creating robust structures. *Visit them at https://llcattorney.com Use CODE: STRATUS25ACT to get your Formation Fees 100% Waived by me.*

3. **Diversify Risk:** Avoid clustering too many properties or assets under a single legal entity. Compartmentalization ensures each asset remains insulated from others in case of a liability claim.

4. **Integrate Trusts for Legacy Planning:** Incorporate irrevocable trusts into your long-term plan to shield assets from creditors and ensure tax-efficient wealth transfer to future generations.

5. **Regularly Review and Update Your Asset Protection Plan:** Your asset protection plan should evolve as your portfolio grows. Periodically review your legal structures to account for new acquisitions, changes in state laws, or shifting personal circumstances.

Recommended Tools for Asset Protection

1. **LLC Attorney:** www.llcattorney.com
    Tailored LLC and Series LLC setups for real estate investors, emphasizing privacy and protection.
    DISCOUNT CODE: STRATUS25ACT

2. **Anderson Advisors:**
   Specializes in real estate asset protection, offering comprehensive guidance on legal structures, equity stripping, and tax strategies.

3. **Trust & Will:**
   Simplifies the creation of living trusts, ideal for investors seeking basic estate planning solutions.

4. **Rocket Lawyer:**
   Provides affordable legal services for drafting basic asset protection documents and contracts.

Asset Protection: The Steel Rebar of Resilience

Asset protection isn't just a defensive strategy—it's a proactive measure to secure your Hard Asset Empire™ against the unpredictable. You build an impenetrable shield around your wealth by combining LLC structures, trusts, equity stripping, and strategic planning.

These measures allow you to weather legal threats, maintain financial stability, and focus on the growth and longevity of your empire. The next section'll explore tax planning—the keystone of wealth optimization and resilience. With both asset protection and tax strategies in place, your financial fortress will be well-equipped to thrive through any challenge.

Tax Planning – The Steel Tightrope That Preserves Wealth

If insurance is the safety net and asset protection is the shield, tax planning is the tightrope that ensures your **Hard Asset Empire™** remains efficient, sustainable, and primed for growth. Taxes, often one of investors' largest expenses, can silently erode wealth when left unchecked. Yet, with strategic planning, tax efficiency becomes a powerful mechanism for preserving capital, compounding growth, and accelerating wealth-building.

Effective tax planning is about proactively managing liabilities rather than reacting at year-end. By leveraging real estate's unique tax advantages, adopting proven wealth-preservation strategies, and partnering with experienced tax advisors, you can retain more of your hard-earned capital and reinvest it into the incremental growth of your empire.

Key Tax Strategies for Investors

Depreciation Benefits: The Hidden Power of Real Estate

One of the most significant tax advantages of real estate investing is **depreciation**—the ability to deduct the gradual "wear and tear" of your property as a business expense. Unlike most other investments, real estate allows you to benefit from paper losses that offset taxable income without impacting cash flow.

Cost Segregation Studies are a powerful tool for investors seeking to maximize depreciation. Cost segregation accelerates depreciation by breaking down a property's components (e.g., fixtures, electrical systems, and HVAC) into shorter depreciation schedules, typically 5, 7, or 15 years instead of the standard 27.5 years for residential or 39 years for commercial properties.

Example:
A $1 million commercial property might yield $200,000 in first-year deductions through a cost segregation study, significantly reducing taxable income from rental cash flow.

Practical Application:

- Conduct cost segregation studies on newly acquired or existing properties.
- Partner with qualified engineers and tax professionals to ensure compliance with IRS regulations.

Tool Recommendation:

- **KBKG**: https://www.kbkg.com/residential-costsegregator Offers comprehensive cost segregation services tailored to residential real estate investors.
- **Segstream** is another software tool that does cost-segregation https://www.segstream.com/
- **Stessa**: https://www.stessa.com/ Tracks depreciation schedules seamlessly as part of your financial reporting and property management software toolkit.

1031 Exchanges: Keep Your Capital Working

A **1031 Exchange**, named after Section 1031 of the IRS tax code, allows investors to defer capital gains taxes when selling one property and reinvesting the proceeds into a "like-kind" asset. This strategy keeps more capital working for you, enabling you to scale your portfolio without taking a tax hit.

The key to executing a successful 1031 Exchange is planning. Strict deadlines apply:

- **45 Days** to identify potential replacement properties.
- **180 Days** to close on the acquisition of the new property.

Example:
An investor sells a multifamily property for $2 million, realizing a $500,000 gain. By reinvesting into a larger mixed-use property via a 1031 Exchange, they defer capital gains taxes while increasing their portfolio's size and cash flow.

Practical Steps:

1. Work with a **qualified intermediary (QI)** to handle the exchange process.
2. Identify replacement properties early to avoid missing deadlines.
3. Use tools like **Crexi** or **CoStar** to source high-potential assets quickly.

Tool Recommendation:

- **IPX1031**: A trusted platform for managing 1031 Exchange transactions.
- **Crexi**: Provides listings and market data for identifying like-kind replacement properties.

Opportunity Zones: Tax-Advantaged Investments for Growth

Opportunity Zones (QOZs) are designated areas across the United States that provide tax incentives for investors to direct capital into underserved communities. Established under the 2017 Tax Cuts and Jobs Act, QOZs offer a trifecta of benefits, and with a Trump 2.0 administration, this tax code will likely be extended or renewed, so keep a close watch on this from 2025 forward:

1. **Tax Deferral**: Capital gains taxes on proceeds reinvested in a QOZ fund are deferred until 2026.
2. **Tax Reduction**: Holding the investment for 5-7 years can reduce your deferred gains tax liability.
3. **Tax-Free Growth**: After 10 years, gains from the Opportunity Zone investment are tax-free.

4. **Example:**

   An investor reinvests $1 million in capital gains into a QOZ project, such as developing a multifamily building. By holding the investment for 10+ years, they not only defer the original tax liability but also benefit from tax-free appreciation.

Practical Steps:

- Identify Opportunity Zone locations using resources like the **Census Opportunity Zone Map**.
- Invest in QOZ funds or projects with strong appreciation and cash flow potential.
- Collaborate with QOZ advisors who specialize in compliance and structuring.

Tool Recommendation:

- **Novogradac**: Provides data and analysis on Opportunity Zone projects.
- **Census Opportunity Zone Map**: Helps investors locate designated QOZs.

Passive Income Tax Strategies: Reducing Taxable Rental Income

Income generated from rental properties is classified as **passive income**, which often benefits from lower tax rates than earned income. By leveraging deductions, investors can further reduce their taxable income, increasing cash flow while maintaining compliance with the IRS.

Key deductions include:

- **Mortgage Interest**: Deduct the interest paid on loans for income-producing properties.
- **Property Taxes**: Fully deductible as a business expense.
- **Repairs and Maintenance**: Costs for routine upkeep can be deducted immediately.
- **Insurance Premiums**: Protecting your properties through insurance provides a tax benefit.
- **Depreciation**: Annual depreciation deductions lower taxable income over the asset's life.

Practical Application:

- Automate expense tracking with tools like **Stessa** or **QuickBooks**.

- Work with a tax advisor to identify additional opportunities for deductions, like renewable energy credits for installing solar panels.

Retirement Accounts for Real Estate: The Tax-Advantaged Play

Self-directed retirement accounts, such as **Self-Directed IRAs** or **Solo 401(k)s**, provide real estate investors with a unique advantage: tax-deferred or tax-free growth on rental income and capital gains.

How It Works:

- **Self-Directed IRAs** allow you to invest in real estate, while income and gains remain tax-deferred until distributions are made in retirement.
- **Solo 401(k)s** offer higher contribution limits and the ability to borrow against the plan for additional investment capital.

Example:
An investor uses $200,000 from a Solo 401(k) to acquire a rental property. The rental income generated grows tax-free

within the account, significantly accelerating wealth accumulation over time.

Practical Steps:

1. Open a Self-Directed IRA or Solo 401(k) with a custodian experienced in real estate.
2. Identify income-producing properties that align with your investment strategy.
3. Use platforms like **Equity Trust** or **Rocket Dollar** to manage and track investments.

Tool Recommendation:

- **Rocket Dollar**: Simplifies the process of opening and managing self-directed retirement accounts.
- **Equity Trust**: Provides custodial services for alternative assets within IRAs and Solo 401(k)s.

Practical Steps for Implementing a Tax Plan

1. **Hire a Real Estate Tax Strategist**: Collaborate with a CPA or tax advisor specializing in real estate to identify and implement tax-saving opportunities. Real estate-specific expertise ensures you leverage every advantage the tax code offers.

2. **Conduct Annual Reviews**: The tax landscape evolves regularly. Schedule annual portfolio reviews to identify new incentives, maximize deductions, and optimize your tax strategy.
3. **Track Expenses and Income**: Use tools like **Stessa** or **QuickBooks** to automate the tracking of rental income, expenses, and deductions. Accurate records are essential for minimizing tax liabilities.
4. **Maximize Tax Incentives**: Stay informed about tax incentives such as renewable energy credits, bonus depreciation, and other programs that can reduce your tax burden.

Recommended Tools for Tax Planning

- **Stessa**: Real estate-specific software for tracking expenses, income, and tax deductions.
- **Rocket Dollar**: Simplifies setting up tax-advantaged accounts like Self-Directed IRAs and Solo 401(k)s.
- **KBKG**: Cost segregation studies for accelerated depreciation.
- **Novogradac**: Comprehensive insights on Opportunity Zones.

- **TaxJar**: Automates tax calculations for complex portfolios with multiple assets.

Tax Efficiency as a Growth Catalyst

Tax planning is among the most powerful tools for building and preserving wealth within your **Hard Asset Empire™**. You can minimize liabilities and reinvest savings into new growth opportunities by strategically leveraging depreciation benefits, 1031 Exchanges, Opportunity Zone incentives, and tax-advantaged retirement accounts.

Taxes are a reality of wealth-building, but they don't have to be a burden. You can turn tax efficiency into a competitive advantage with the right strategies, tools, and expert advisors. By walking the tightrope of proactive planning, you ensure your empire remains resilient, sustainable, and primed for future success..

The steel-strong reinforcements of **insurance, asset protection, and tax planning** ensure that your financial fortress doesn't just stand tall—it stands **strong**. While the bricks, mortar, and keystones give your empire its form, this resilience framework delivers long-term durability, shielding your wealth from economic storms, personal challenges, and financial threats.

Resilience, like the steel that reinforces a structure, provides **confidence**. It allows you to remain steady when others are forced to retreat, creating an undeniable advantage. By layering your fortress with thoughtful insurance policies, bulletproof asset protection strategies, and efficient tax planning, you insulate your empire against unexpected hits and build a system of recovery that turns setbacks into opportunities.

However, resilience is more than just protection—it's a mindset. Resilient investors aren't reactive; they anticipate challenges and fortify their position **before** trouble arises. With these mechanisms in place, you're not just building for today—you're building a fortress that will endure **for generations**. This is how legacies are created: not by hoping for the best, but by preparing for anything.

Looking Ahead: Legacy and Vision

Your Hard Asset Empire™ is not just about accumulating wealth—it's about ensuring that wealth serves a **greater purpose**. In the next chapter, we enter the final phase of your blueprint: **Legacy and Vision**. Here, you'll learn how to **preserve, transfer, and expand your impact** across generations. From estate planning and philanthropic endeavors to creating systems that sustain your family's vision for decades to come, we'll focus on how to put the finishing capstones on your fortress.

The result? A financial empire that doesn't just survive—but thrives—and one that tells a story of purpose, prosperity, and enduring impact. **Let's turn to the final pieces of your blueprint and prepare your legacy for the future.**

Endnotes

1. Hub International, "Commercial Real Estate Insurance Solutions," https://www.hubinternational.com/.
2. The Hartford, "Business Insurance Tailored for Real Estate Owners," https://www.thehartford.com/.
3. Riskalyze, "Risk Management and Portfolio Assessment Tools," https://www.riskalyze.com/.
4. Wyoming LLC Attorney, "LLC and Series LLC Asset Protection Solutions," https://wyomingllcattorney.com/.
5. Anderson Advisors, *Asset Protection for Real Estate Investors*, https://andersonadvisors.com/.
6. Trust & Will, "Simplified Estate Planning and Trust Creation," https://trustandwill.com/.
7. Rocket Lawyer, "Affordable Legal Document Solutions," https://www.rocketlawyer.com/.
8. Federal Emergency Management Agency (FEMA), "Natural Disaster Risk Assessments," https://www.fema.gov/.
9. Prophia, "Lease Analytics and Market Data for Asset Optimization," https://www.prophia.com/.
10. Juniper Square, "Investor and Partnership Management Tools," https://www.junipersquare.com/.
11. Legal Information Institute, "Homestead Exemption Laws by State," Cornell Law School, https://www.law.cornell.edu/wex/homestead_exemption.
12. IRS, "Tax Exemptions and Irrevocable Trusts," https://www.irs.gov/.
13. Bankrate, "How Umbrella Insurance Works," https://www.bankrate.com/.
14. National Multifamily Housing Council (NMHC), "Managing Risk in Multifamily Real Estate," https://www.nmhc.org/.

15. Harvard Business Review, "The Role of Insurance in Resilience Strategies," https://hbr.org/.
16. U.S. Small Business Administration (SBA), "Business Interruption Insurance Guidance," https://www.sba.gov/.
17. CoStar Group, "Trends in Commercial Property Insurance," https://www.costar.com/.
18. Yardi Voyager, "Property Management and Risk Mitigation Tools," https://www.yardi.com/.
19. Bloomberg Terminal, "Macroeconomic and Geopolitical Risk Analysis," https://www.bloomberg.com/professional/.
20. RealPage, "Asset Performance and Insurance Analytics," https://www.realpage.com/.

SECTION 3:

Legacy and Vision

7

The Capstones: Adaptability, Legacy, and Vision

Building your Hard Asset Empire™ is much like constructing a grand architectural marvel. Every element contributes to its strength and durability, from the solid foundation to the resilient steel framing. Yet, even the most formidable structures require *capstones—the finishing touches that bring cohesion, distinction, and purpose to the entire design*. Capstones represent adaptability, legacy, fun, and vision in the blueprint of your financial fortress. These elements ensure that your empire not only endures but also leaves a lasting impact for generations to come, and that it is infused with your personal style and family values that will be a sense of pride for your future generations.

The capstones are about more than wealth; they are about purpose—how you adapt to change, transfer wealth effectively, and extend your influence through philanthropy. A fortress without capstones may still stand, but it will lack refinement and the generational story that elevates it from mere wealth to a meaningful legacy.

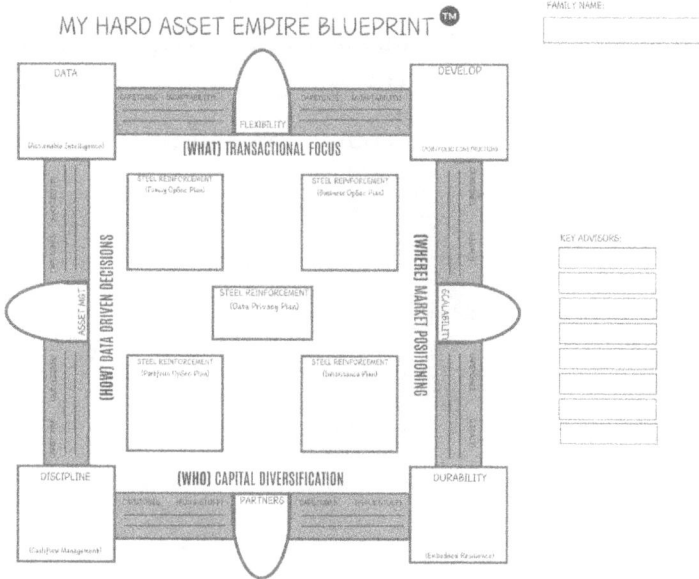

MY HARD ASSET EMPIRE BLUEPRINT ™

Adaptability: The Finishing Touch That Preserves the Empire

Adaptability is a critical quality in both investing and leadership. In a constantly evolving economic landscape, the ability to pivot, innovate, and respond to change ensures that your Hard Asset Empire™ remains resilient and relevant.

History teaches us that those who refuse to adapt are often the first to crumble. Whether due to technological disruption, economic downturns, or shifting generational values, the unprepared empire risks obsolescence. Adaptability is the capstone that locks everything else in place, allowing your fortress to withstand new challenges and thrive under changing circumstances.

MY HARD ASSET EMPIRE BLUEPRINT™

FAMILY NAME:

DATA

DEVELOP

FLEXIBILITY

(Actionable Intelligence)

(WHAT) TRANSACTIONAL FOCUS

(Portfolio Construction)

CAPSTONES ADAPTABILITY

STEEL REINFORCEMENT
(Family Option Plan)

STEEL REINFORCEMENT
(Business Option Plan)

STEEL REINFORCEMENT
(Data Privacy Plan)

STEEL REINFORCEMENT
(Portfolio Option Plan)

STEEL REINFORCEMENT
(Inheritance Plan)

(HOW) DATA DRIVEN DECISIONS

(WHERE) MARKET POSITIONING

ASSET MGT

SCALABILITY

DISCIPLINE

DURABILITY

(Cash Flow Management)

(WHO) CAPITAL DIVERSIFICATION

(Embedded Resilience)

PARTNERS

CAPSTONES (FUN & STUFF)

CAPSTONES (FUN & STUFF)

KEY ADVISORS:

The Role of Adaptability in Your Blueprint

Adaptability is not about abandoning your principles but refining your strategies. For example, as economic environments shift, an investor might pivot from office properties to industrial warehouses to capitalize on the rise of e-commerce. Similarly, technological advancements may allow you to integrate artificial intelligence (AI) tools to streamline operations, harness data-driven insights, and find efficiencies where none previously existed.

Practical Examples:

- Market Shifts: During the COVID-19 pandemic, many investors with heavy exposure to retail properties were forced to adapt. Some transformed struggling retail spaces into last-mile distribution centers, while others reimagined them as mixed-use facilities with residential and commercial tenants.
- Technological Advancements: AI tools like ATOMIQ's nBrain™ offer investors a "central nervous system" for their empire. With Retrieval-Augmented Generation (RAG) models, nBrain can aggregate data from multiple sources, predict market trends, and suggest actionable investment opportunities. This kind of intelligence allows empires to adapt with precision.

- Generational Change: Millennials and Gen Z prioritize sustainable investments and environmental, social, and governance (ESG) initiatives. By adapting to this shift, you can secure tenant demand and align with long-term market trends.

Steps to Building Adaptability

1. Monitor Trends: Stay ahead of macroeconomic, demographic, and technological trends using tools like Bloomberg Terminal, CoStar, and Prophia.
2. Embrace Technology: Integrate adaptable systems that centralize operations, harness actionable intelligence, and automate routine tasks.
3. Stress-Test Your Portfolio: Regularly assess your investments for vulnerabilities and opportunities to pivot toward stronger asset classes.
4. Build Liquidity Buffers: Maintain enough liquidity to respond to unexpected changes or capitalize on sudden opportunities.

War Stories from the Alliance Vault:

The Capstone Crisis: How I Almost Missed the Opportunity to Leave a Legacy

When I first considered investing in the medical sector, the market was a maze of uncertainty. The healthcare landscape was shifting, regulations were unpredictable, and the economic climate made long-term commitments feel like high-stakes gambles. I was at a crossroads—dive into a sector I didn't fully understand or stick to the commercial properties I knew like the back of my hand.

I decided to sit down with a group of key investors and industry experts. I wasn't looking for hype; I was looking for substance. Where should we be investing? What would remain viable in an uncertain future? Through those conversations, we stumbled upon dialysis centers. The more I learned, the more the logic behind it clicked.

Kidney dialysis isn't a luxury. It's a necessity. Millions of Americans require treatment multiple times per week. The demand wasn't going anywhere—it was only increasing. Unlike other medical trends that rise and fall with advancements in technology, dialysis remained a constant. The human body was never going out of style, and for many, dialysis was the lifeline keeping them alive.

With that revelation, I dug deeper into the medical real estate sector. I realized that, unlike retail stores or office buildings, medical offices don't relocate easily. Doctors spend years building a clientele, and their location becomes a part of their professional stability. That stability translates into long-term security for investors like me.

Had I ignored the opportunity, I would have missed one of the most lucrative and sustainable investment plays of my career. Instead, I embraced it, knowing that my investments in medical real estate weren't just about returns—they were about creating something lasting. The stability of these properties meant steady cash flow, long-term tenant retention, and an asset class that could withstand economic turbulence.

Lessons Learned

1. **Find Stability in Essential Markets** – The medical sector provided long-term security because it serves fundamental human needs that don't change with trends.
2. **Look Beyond the Present** – While others hesitated, I leaned into an investment strategy that secured lasting returns.
3. **Long-Term Thinking Wins** – The best investments—whether in real estate or in family—are built on foresight and discipline.

By taking calculated risks, listening to the right voices, and ensuring the next generation understood what it takes to sustain wealth, I built a foundation that won't just last for my lifetime, but for generations to come and with your *Hard Asset Empire Blueprint*™ you can now do the same thing and use it as a document to hold discussions with your family members and key advisors in a concise way to help ensure your vision can be expanded by the next generation as they apply their own vision on top of its solid foundation.

Adaptability is often the difference between survival and collapse. Your ability to pivot—whether by reallocating capital, integrating new technologies, or changing investment strategies—will determine the long-term success of your empire.

Legacy Planning Capstones: Making an Impact Beyond Your Walls

A key measure of your **Hard Asset Empire™** is its ability to outlive you. Legacy planning ensures that the wealth you've worked so hard to build is preserved, protected, and effectively transferred to future generations. However, wealth transfer is rarely straightforward—it requires careful planning to avoid unnecessary taxes, legal disputes, and family dynamics that can tear an empire apart.

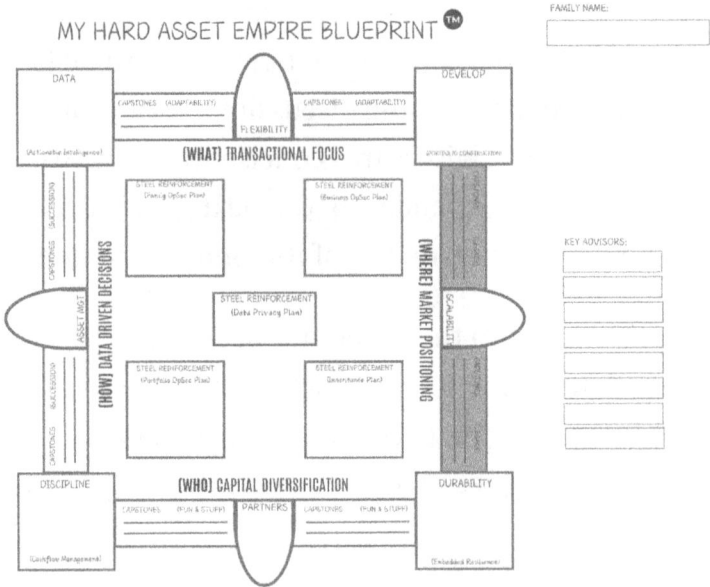

The Challenge of Legacy Planning

The old saying, "Shirtsleeves to shirtsleeves in three generations," highlights a sobering reality: most family wealth is lost by the third generation. The reasons are varied—poor communication, a lack of financial education, and unprepared heirs—but the root cause is often a failure to plan.

Legacy planning involves more than just dividing assets; it's about instilling values, creating systems, and preparing the next generation to carry the torch responsibly. Without this, even the most impressive empires can disintegrate.

Philanthropy: Expanding Your Impact Beyond Wealth

The final capstone in your blueprint is philanthropy. True legacies are not measured solely by financial wealth but by their impact on the world. Philanthropy allows you to extend your influence, create meaningful change, and instill values in your family that transcend generations.

For many, philanthropy represents the culmination of their success—the opportunity to give back and leave the world better than they found it. Whether through charitable giving, foundation creation, or community initiatives, philanthropy can serve as a powerful tool for purpose-driven wealth.

The Benefits of Philanthropy

1. Purpose and Fulfillment: Giving back creates a sense of purpose, aligning wealth with personal values.
2. Tax Advantages: Charitable donations often provide significant tax deductions, reducing taxable income while supporting causes you care about.

3. Strengthening Family Bonds: Philanthropy can unite families around shared values and missions, fostering cooperation and purpose across generations.
4. Creating a Legacy of Impact: Foundations, endowments, or charitable initiatives carry your name and values forward, creating a lasting imprint.

Key Strategies for Philanthropy

1. Donor-Advised Funds (DAFs): DAFs allow you to contribute assets, receive immediate tax benefits, and recommend grants to charities over time.
2. Private Foundations: Establishing a family foundation gives you greater control over how funds are distributed and allows for multi-generational involvement.
3. Charitable Trusts: Charitable remainder trusts (CRTs) and charitable lead trusts (CLTs) provide tax-efficient ways to donate assets while maintaining income streams for beneficiaries.
4. Impact Investing: Invest in businesses or projects that generate financial returns while achieving positive social or environmental outcomes.

Practical Example: The Giving Pledge

The Giving Pledge, spearheaded by Warren Buffett and Bill Gates, encourages billionaires to commit at least half their wealth to philanthropy. While you may not have billions to give, the principle remains the same: align your wealth with your values and make a difference.

Philanthropy is not about the size of the gift—it's about the impact. Whether funding a local school, supporting medical research, or helping an underserved community, your giving can leave an enduring legacy.

Building a Legacy That Stands the Test of Time

The capstones of adaptability, legacy, and vision elevate your Hard Asset Empire™ beyond financial success. They transform your wealth into a force for purpose, continuity, and impact. By staying adaptable, planning for an effective wealth transfer, and embracing philanthropy, you ensure that your fortress stands strong for your lifetime and for generations to come.

Practical Steps to Implement Capstones

3. **Philanthropy:** Align your wealth with causes that matter to you by creating donor-advised funds, family foundations, or impact investing initiatives. Involve your heirs in these efforts to teach them the value of stewardship and contribution.

4. **Regular Reviews:** A fortress isn't built once—it requires maintenance and occasional upgrades. Revisit your adaptability strategies, estate plans, and philanthropic efforts regularly to ensure they align with your current circumstances and future goals.

5. **Engage Experts:** Don't attempt to go it alone. Work with trusted advisors such as estate planners, tax strategists, and philanthropic consultants to refine and optimize your capstone strategies.

Key Strategies for Legacy Planning

1. Establish an Estate Plan: Work with professionals to set up wills, trusts, and other vehicles that efficiently transfer wealth while minimizing estate taxes.

- Irrevocable Trusts: Protect assets from creditors, lawsuits, and estate taxes.
- Dynasty Trusts: Preserve wealth for multiple generations while reducing tax exposure.
- Living Trusts: Provide a seamless transfer of assets without probate delays.
- *Recommended Resource:* _Wyoming LLC Attorney_—a resource for creating protective LLCs and trusts.

2. Create a Family Governance Structure: Establish guidelines for how future generations will manage and use wealth. Formal family offices can centralize wealth management, financial education, and decision-making.

  - Family Meetings: Hold regular meetings to align on family values, responsibilities, and investment decisions.
  - Mission Statements: Develop a family mission statement that defines the purpose of the wealth and the vision for future generations

3. Prepare Heirs Through Financial Education: The best way to ensure wealth survives is to teach the next generation how to manage it. Financial literacy

programs, mentorship, and real-world asset management involvement are essential.

Succession Planning Capstones: The Fragile Nature of Wealth Transfer

We've all seen it—families that spend generations building wealth, only to see it disappear within a lifetime. The data is sobering: nearly 70% of wealthy families lose their wealth by the second generation, and 90% lose it by the third. Why? Because wealth alone isn't enough. Without a structured, well-executed succession plan, the very assets that took a lifetime to build can become burdens that unravel everything.

True succession planning isn't just about passing down assets; it's about passing down wisdom, principles, and discipline. A Hard Asset Empire isn't just a portfolio—it's a structure, a philosophy, and a blueprint to ensure that future generations are equipped to sustain and grow what has been built.

MY HARD ASSET EMPIRE BLUEPRINT ™

DATA

DEVELOP

CAPSTONES (ADAPTABILITY)   CAPSTONES (ADAPTABILITY)

FLEXIBILITY

(WHAT) TRANSACTIONAL FOCUS

(Actionable Intelligence)

PORTFOLIO CONSTRUCTION

STEEL REINFORCEMENT
(Trading Cycles Plan)

STEEL REINFORCEMENT
(Business Cycles Plan)

KEY ADVISORS:

(HOW) DATA DRIVEN DECISIONS

ASSET MGT

SCALABILITY

STEEL REINFORCEMENT
(Data Privacy Plan)

(WHERE) MARKET POSITIONING

STEEL REINFORCEMENT
(Portfolio Cycles Plan)

STEEL REINFORCEMENT
(Succession Plan)

DISCIPLINE

DURABILITY

(WHO) CAPITAL DIVERSIFICATION

CAPSTONES (FUN & STUFF)   PARTNERS   CAPSTONES (FUN & STUFF)

(Cashflow Management)

(Embedded Resilience)

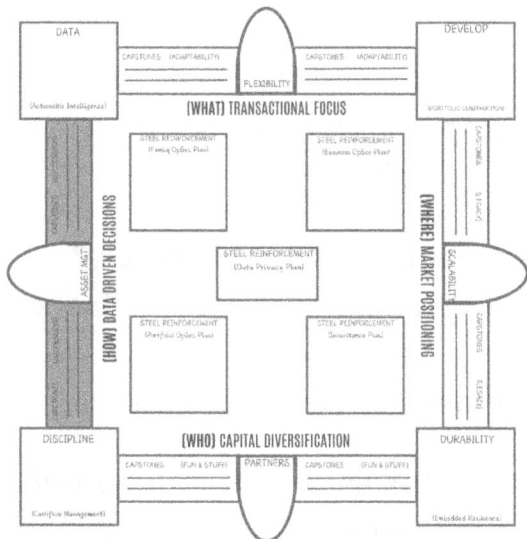

The Succession Planning Blueprint

To successfully transfer wealth and leadership without crippling the next generation, a structured framework is essential. Here's the Hard Asset Empire Blueprint™ for succession:

1. Define the Core Values and Mission of the Family Enterprise

Before you think about handing over assets, you need to establish the guiding principles that define the family's financial philosophy. This includes:

- **What does wealth mean to your family?**
- **What are the guiding values behind financial decisions?**
- **How does wealth serve a larger purpose?**

If there is no shared vision, then financial assets will be treated as individual windfalls rather than a collective legacy.

2. Educate Before You Entrust

Too many successors inherit wealth before they inherit financial literacy. The key to preventing entitlement and mismanagement is education. This education must be ongoing and experiential:

- **Start Early:** Teach children the basics of earning, saving, and investing from a young age.
- **Real-World Application:** Allow heirs to manage portions of assets under guidance, such as running a family-owned property or participating in investment decisions.

- **Mentorship:** Assign mentors from within or outside the family to prepare the next generation for stewardship roles.

3. Leverage the Three-Tiered Asset Protection Model

A structured succession plan needs protective layers to preserve the core estate while allowing beneficiaries to grow and innovate. The three-tiered asset protection model ensures that wealth is structured correctly:

- **Operating Entities:** Income-generating assets should be held in separate legal entities, such as LLCs or limited partnerships, to shield personal wealth from business risks.
- **Family Trusts:** These provide tax advantages, protection from lawsuits, and a structured distribution plan to prevent reckless spending.
- **Investment Pools:** Set up diversified investment pools that balance risk and long-term growth, ensuring sustained wealth over multiple generations.

4. Implement Governance Structures That Outlast Any One Generation

A Hard Asset Empire isn't just a business—it's an institution. Institutions require governance. Without rules and oversight, family wealth becomes individual fortunes, which tend to shrink over time. Effective governance structures include:

- **Family Councils:** A governing body that makes strategic financial and business decisions.
- **Advisory Boards:** Non-family advisors who ensure professional management and prevent conflicts of interest.
- **Succession Committees:** A formal process for leadership transition, ensuring smooth handovers of decision-making power.

5. Create Performance-Based Wealth Access

One of the biggest mistakes in wealth transfer is making financial independence too easy. When heirs receive wealth without accountability, ambition diminishes. Instead of handing out lump sums, structure wealth access based on performance and responsibility:

- **Milestone-Based Distributions:** Heirs access funds only after reaching financial literacy milestones, earning degrees, or proving business acumen.
- **Investment Matching Programs:** For every dollar an heir invests wisely, the family estate matches it.

- **Mandatory Work Experience:** Before taking leadership roles, heirs must gain experience outside the family business to develop skills and resilience.

Tying Succession Capstones into the Hard Asset Empire Blueprint™

The Hard Asset Empire Blueprint™ isn't just about accumulating wealth—it's about sustaining and growing it through a multi-generational approach. Some example capstones you could borrow or customize and be inspired by are what hold your empire together through the generations:

Capstone #1: Wealth as a Stewardship, Not an Ownership

The family wealth is a trust that each generation stewards for the next. Viewing it this way eliminates entitlement and fosters responsibility.

Capstone #2: Structure Before Emotion

Families that mix emotional decisions with financial ones suffer losses. A structured plan prevents family dynamics from eroding financial stability.

Capstone #3: Built to Last, Not Just to Spend

A Hard Asset Empire™ isn't about enjoying the wealth of the previous generation; it's about ensuring that wealth continues to compound into the future while you enjoy the fruits of it today.

Capstone #4: Adaptive, Not Rigid

Markets change. Economies shift. The best succession plans are flexible, allowing for adaptation while holding to core values.

The True Measure of Success

A successful succession plan is one where future generations don't just inherit wealth—they inherit the mindset, discipline, and tools to sustain it. With the Hard Asset Empire Blueprint, wealth is not just a number; it's a system designed to endure.

The true measure of success isn't just how much is passed down, but how long it lasts and how much impact it creates. That's the power of structured succession planning.

War Stories from the Alliance Vault

The Torchbearer's Dilemma: Lessons in Wealth Transfer and Family Dynamics

Building wealth is one challenge; preserving it across generations is another. I've seen too many fortunes built in one generation and squandered in the next. I didn't want that to be my family's story. That's why, when my kids hit high school, I implemented a financial discipline experiment that shaped their understanding of money for life.

They were each given an allowance—not a free ride, but a structured monthly budget that covered their essential needs: gas, food, and a few basics. It started at $100 per month, and the rules were simple. That money had to last. If they burned through it in the first two weeks, they had to figure it out.

I watched as they made decisions that mirrored real-world financial constraints. They quickly realized that eating out every day would drain their funds. They learned to coordinate rides with friends to save gas money. They discovered that borrowing and lending between each other required trust and accountability.

Most importantly, they began to understand the value of a dollar—not just in terms of what it could buy, but in terms of opportunity cost. Every expense became a decision, and every decision carried consequences.

This lesson wasn't just about budgeting; it was about building financial awareness and responsibility. It was about making sure that when the time came to pass the torch, they would be prepared to carry it, not just receive it.

Wealth without wisdom is a burden. Legacy planning ensures that your heirs inherit not only your assets but also the principles and tools they need to sustain and grow them.

Wealth Must Be Taught, Not Just Given – *By instilling financial responsibility early, my kids gained the skills to manage wealth rather than simply inherit it.*

Fun & Stuff Capstones: The Purpose of Wealth Beyond Security

Wealth isn't just about surviving hard times—*it's also about creating great times.* Too many people build their financial empires around fear, focusing solely on preservation without fully embracing the enjoyment wealth can bring. A truly wealthy life isn't one spent hoarding assets in preparation for disaster; it balances protection with celebration, knowing that security isn't just about defense, but about the ability to create joy, freedom, and unforgettable experiences regardless of external circumstances.

A Hard Asset Empire™ isn't just about legacy—it's about lifestyle. It should provide for future generations and the quality of life you and your family can enjoy today.

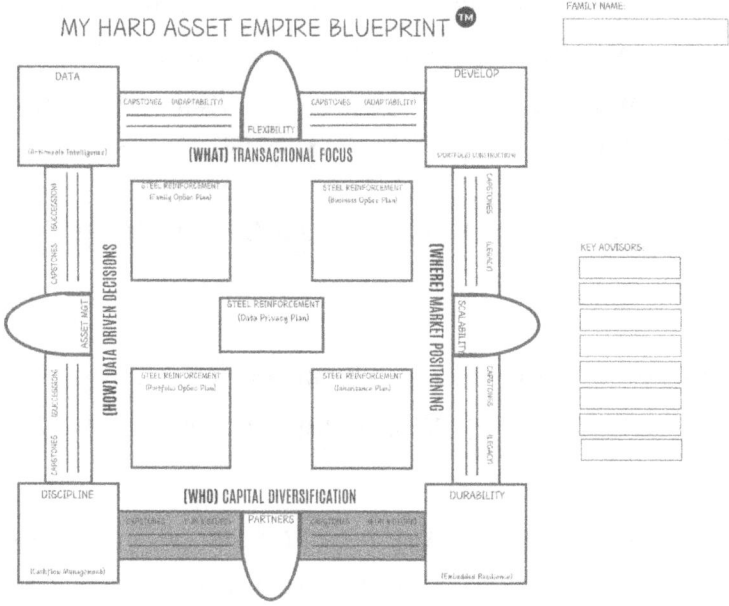

MY HARD ASSET EMPIRE BLUEPRINT™

FAMILY NAME:

DATA | DEVELOP

CAPSTONES (ADAPTABILITY) — CAPSTONES (ADAPTABILITY)

FLEXIBILITY

(WHAT) TRANSACTIONAL FOCUS

(Artificial Intelligence) | (Portfolio Construction)

STEEL REINFORCEMENT (Family Office Plan) | STEEL REINFORCEMENT (Business Option Plan)

KEY ADVISORS

(HOW) DATA DRIVEN DECISIONS

ASSET MGT

STEEL REINFORCEMENT (Data Privacy Plan)

(WHERE) MARKET POSITIONING

SCALABILITY

STEEL REINFORCEMENT (Portfolio Option Plan) | STEEL REINFORCEMENT (Governance Plan)

DISCIPLINE | (WHO) CAPITAL DIVERSIFICATION | DURABILITY

PARTNERS

(Cash flow Management) | (Embedded Resilience)

The Enjoyment Planning Blueprint

True financial mastery includes a plan for enjoyment, just as much as a plan for investment and security. Here's the Hard Asset Empire Blueprint™ for making the most of wealth while ensuring it remains sustainable:

1. Define What Enjoyment Means to You and Your Family

Luxury means different things to different people. For some, it's owning high-end assets. For others, it's the ability to travel the world, experience new cultures, and create memories. And for many, it's about freedom—the ability to say yes to opportunities without hesitation. Define what truly brings fulfillment so that your wealth fuels experiences that align with your values, not just impulsive spending.

2. Build an Enjoyment Fund Just Like an Investment Fund

Just as every portfolio has allocations for different assets, your financial strategy should include allocations for fun and experiences.

- **Experiences Fund:** A designated portion of your earnings should be set aside for once-in-a-lifetime experiences—travel, concerts, sporting events, adventures.
- **Luxury Asset Fund:** If material possessions bring you joy, structure purchases wisely. Instead of depreciating assets that drain cash flow, invest in tangible assets that retain or appreciate in value.

- **Philanthropic Giving:** True enjoyment comes not just from acquiring but also from giving. Create impact-driven funds for charitable experiences that align with your family's vision.

3. Incorporate Celebration Into Your Family Wealth Culture

Enjoyment isn't just about spending money—it's about fostering a culture of celebration. Families that build wealth without joy often create future generations that resent the burden of preservation. Ensure that luxury and lifestyle aren't just afterthoughts but integral to how your wealth functions.

- **Ritualized Celebrations:** Annual retreats, milestone trips, and memorable family events should be built into your wealth structure.
- **Exclusive Experiences:** Leverage your financial position to create access to experiences money alone can't buy—private events, personalized adventures, unique gatherings that deepen family bonds.
- **Personalized Legacy Spending:** Create funds for family members to pursue passions, whether that's collecting art, sailing, culinary experiences, or learning from world-class mentors.

4. Acquire Luxury With Intention, Not Impulse

There's a difference between reckless spending and strategic luxury. The key is ensuring that indulgence fits into the larger wealth-building plan.

- **Cash Flow-Generating Assets:** Exotic cars, yachts, and vacation homes can be structured as income-generating assets rather than liabilities. Understand how to offset costs through rental programs, fractional ownership, and tax-efficient structures.
- **Art and Collectibles:** Luxury assets like fine art, rare watches, and collectible automobiles provide personal enjoyment and can also appreciate in value when selected wisely.
- **Experience-Based Spending:** Rather than simply accumulating material possessions, prioritize experiences that create memories and personal fulfillment.

5. Live on Offense, Not Just Defense

A Hard Asset Empire™ isn't just built to weather storms—it's designed to thrive in any environment. That means structuring your life to ensure joy, adventure, and fulfillment no matter what's happening in the broader economy.

- **Economic Independence Means Freedom:** When your wealth is structured to withstand economic downturns, you retain the power to live life on your terms.
- **Master the Art of Splurging Without Guilt:** True financial security allows for enjoyment without fear. When your foundation is solid, there's no reason not to embrace the best life offers.
- **Celebrate Wins Along the Way:** Too many people delay gratification until retirement or an arbitrary financial milestone. A truly wealthy life is one where the rewards are built into the journey, not just saved for the destination.

Tying Enjoyment into the Hard Asset Empire Blueprint Capstones

The Hard Asset Empire Blueprint isn't just about accumulating and protecting wealth—it's about living a truly abundant life. These example capstones below will help you customize yours further to reinforce the importance of enjoying wealth while maintaining its longevity, include:

Capstone #1: Joy Is a Key Metric of Success

A financial plan that doesn't account for joy is an incomplete plan. Sustainable wealth isn't just about preservation—it's about making life richer in every sense.

Capstone #2: Build in Celebration, Not Just Sacrifice

Too many entrepreneurs and investors fall into the trap of endless accumulation without ever enjoying the fruits of their labor. A balanced approach ensures that both security and joy are prioritized.

Capstone #3: Buy Time and Freedom, Not Just Things

The best luxury is time—time to do what you love, with whom you love, on your own terms. Structuring wealth to create time freedom is the ultimate form of success.

Capstone #4: Make Every Dollar Work for Your Happiness

Every financial decision should align with your definition of fulfillment. That means investing not just for returns, but for life-enhancing experiences that truly matter.

The Art of Enjoying Wealth While Preserving It

A successful wealth strategy isn't one that only ensures survival—it's one that ensures a life well-lived. The Hard Asset Empire Blueprint™ isn't just about safeguarding what you've built; it's about leveraging it to create the kind of life most people only dream of. True financial mastery means knowing how to enjoy, celebrate, and thrive, no matter what's happening in the outside world.

The best legacies aren't just about what you leave behind. They're about the life you create while you're here.

The capstones — **adaptability, legacy planning, philanthropy, and fun**—represent the finishing touches that give your Hard Asset Empire™ distinction, purpose, and longevity. These elements ensure that your financial fortress stands as a testament to your success and a beacon of impact, continuity, and resilience.

Adaptability allows your empire to weather economic, technological, and social disruptions. Legacy planning ensures that your wealth—and the principles that created it—are passed on seamlessly to future generations. Philanthropy amplifies your success by creating a positive and lasting influence on the world around you.

Building a financial fortress isn't just about accumulating assets; it's about creating a blueprint that can withstand the test of time and extend its benefits far beyond your lifetime. The capstones are what elevate your empire from wealth to **legacy**, ensuring it stands strong, purposeful, and impactful for generations to come.

Now you have all the framework's elements to complete your customized Hard Asset Empire™ blueprint. In the next section, we'll round out your specified knowledge with some deeper dives on some of the key topics mentioned thus fare as we help you explore the real-world tactics and systems you can look into for executing your wealth creation and generational transfer plan—turning your blueprint into a living, breathing reality that endures for your family and community.

Endnotes

1. Warren Buffett and Bill Gates, *The Giving Pledge*, https://givingpledge.org.
2. Robert T. Kiyosaki and Sharon Lechter, *Rich Dad's Guide to Investing: What the Rich Invest in, That the Poor and Middle Class Do Not* (Plata Publishing, 2012), 58–60.
3. Thomas J. Stanley and William D. Danko, *The Millionaire Next Door: The Surprising Secrets of America's Wealthy* (Taylor Trade Publishing, 1996), 118–120.
4. Charles Duhigg, *The Power of Habit: Why We Do What We Do in Life and Business* (Random House, 2012), 212–215.
5. Thomas J. Anderson, *The Value of Debt in Building Wealth* (Wiley, 2016), 74–76.
6. Bill Gates, "Giving Back: Why Philanthropy Matters," GatesNotes.
7. Bloomberg Terminal, "Global Wealth Trends: Impact of Generational Transfers," Bloomberg.com.
8. KPMG, "Strategic Philanthropy for Family Offices," https://home.kpmg.
9. The Rockefeller Foundation, *Generational Wealth Transfer Strategies*, https://rockefellerfoundation.org.
10. Anderson Advisors, "Legacy Planning and Trust Strategies for Real Estate Investors," https://andersonadvisors.com.
11. Wyoming LLC Attorney, "Using Trusts and LLCs for Asset and Legacy Protection," https://wyomingllcattorney.com.
12. Thomas M. Nichols, *The Death of Expertise: The Campaign Against Established Knowledge* (Oxford University Press, 2017), 150–152.
13. Larry Fink, "The Purpose of a Company: Creating Long-Term Value," *BlackRock Investor Letter*, https://blackrock.com.
14. *Forbes*, "Family Wealth Preservation: The Power of Family Governance Structures," https://www.forbes.com.
15. Vanguard Group, *Investing for Generations: A Guide to Multi-Generational Wealth Transfer*, https://investor.vanguard.com.
16. Internal Revenue Service, "Tax Benefits for Charitable Contributions," https://www.irs.gov.
17. Prophia, "Market Trends and the Evolution of Commercial Real Estate Data," https://prophia.com.
18. Juniper Square, "Optimizing Family Office and Foundation Management," https://junipersquare.com.

SECTION 4:

Deep Dives on Applied Hard Asset Empire™ Strategies

8

Advanced Strategies—Balancing Debt, Equity, and ABL

The walls of your financial fortress must be built with precision. For a Hard Asset Empire™, the strength of those walls comes from a strategic balance of equity-based hard assets, income-generating debt instruments, and asset-based lending (ABL). Together, these elements provide resilience, growth, and predictable cash flow, creating a structure that can endure market volatility and capitalize on opportunities.

However, for sophisticated investors, funds, or family offices, balancing these capital allocations involves more than a basic diversification plan. It requires data-driven strategies, advanced tools, and an ability to assess risks and returns precisely. Leveraging technology, macroeconomic data, and financial modeling ensures that every capital allocation decision adds value to your empire.

This chapter provides advanced strategies for integrating debt, equity, and asset-based lending, along with tools and practical steps to optimize your portfolio.

The Role of Equity-Based Investments: Long-Term Growth and Wealth

Equity-based investments are the cornerstone of any wealth-building portfolio, anchoring your Hard Asset Empire™ with long-term growth, consistent cash flow, and opportunities to create value. These investments, centered around **hard assets** like commercial real estate, industrial facilities, medical office buildings, and multifamily housing, provide the stability and upside that underpin generational wealth. When executed strategically, equity investments outpace inflation, generate recurring income, and act as the financial bedrock of your portfolio.

Equity isn't just about purchasing properties or acquiring shares—it's about **allocating capital with purpose**, balancing risk and reward, and leveraging data to uncover opportunities others miss. For sophisticated investors, family offices, and institutional funds, equity investing requires a nuanced approach to **geographic diversification, sector**

alignment, and **value creation** that ensures long-term success.

Why Equity Investments Matter

1. **Appreciation Potential**
   Appreciation is one of the most powerful advantages of equity-based investments. Hard assets like commercial real estate naturally increase in value over time, driven by macroeconomic forces such as **population growth, urbanization**, and **job creation**. For family offices and institutional investors, appreciation is amplified when paired with value-add strategies like lease optimization, renovations, and operational improvements.

   - **Example:** A Class B industrial warehouse near a major transportation hub in Dallas can appreciate significantly as tenant demand surges due to increased e-commerce activity. Improvements like energy-efficient lighting or adding a tenant improvement allowance can further drive asset value.

2. **Cash Flow Generation**
   Equity investments generate consistent cash flow
   through **rents, leases, or operational income**,
   providing liquidity for reinvestment, debt coverage, or
   new acquisitions. Sectors like **multifamily housing**
   and **medical office buildings** are particularly
   attractive because of their resilience and reliable
   demand.

   Cash flow isn't just a return for sophisticated
   investors—it's a tool. Predictable rental income can be
   used to cover interest obligations on leverage, fund
   renovations, or reinvest into high-growth assets,
   creating a self-sustaining growth cycle.

3. **Control Over Performance**
   Unlike passive investments in paper assets,
   equity-based hard assets offer investors **direct control**
   over outcomes. This control allows investors to create
   value proactively by implementing strategic decisions
   around:

- Operational Efficiencies: Reducing costs and improving management workflows.
- Capital Improvements: Renovations, modernizations, and tenant-focused upgrades.
- Lease Optimization: Aligning rents with market demand, improving tenant mix, or negotiating favorable long-term leases.

4. For example, a value-add multifamily project may involve upgrading kitchens, adding amenities like fitness centers, or introducing smart home technology. These changes boost rents, increase NOI (Net Operating Income), and enhance asset valuation.

Advanced Best Practices for Equity Allocation

Equity allocation must be approached with precision and data-driven insights for family offices and sophisticated investors managing larger portfolios. Here are some strategies to maximize returns:

1. **Diversify Across Sectors and Geographies**
   Diversification is a foundational risk-mitigation strategy. Spread your capital across asset classes that

complement each other:

- **Multifamily Housing**: Resilient during downturns and driven by population growth.
- **Industrial Assets**: Thriving due to the e-commerce boom and demand for logistics hubs.
- **Medical Office Buildings (MOBs)**: Steady returns supported by long-term healthcare demand.

2. Geographic diversification further reduces risk by insulating your portfolio from localized economic disruptions. Tools like **CoStar, Reonomy,** and **ESRI** provide invaluable geospatial and demographic data to pinpoint emerging markets.

3. **Leverage Geospatial and Demographic Data**
   Modern investing requires precision. Platforms like **CoStar** and **Reonomy** analyze macro and microeconomic factors such as:

   - **Population Growth**: Indicates housing demand for multifamily assets.

- Infrastructure Expansion: Points to opportunities in industrial and commercial spaces.
- Employment Trends: Predicts tenant demand in office and retail sectors.

4. For example, data might reveal secondary markets like **Charlotte** or **Boise** as hotspots for population growth and job creation, making them ideal targets for multifamily or industrial acquisitions.

5. **Focus on Value-Add and Opportunistic Deals**
Value-add strategies offer outsized returns by transforming underperforming assets into income-producing powerhouses. Tools like **Prophia** and **Juniper Square** allow investors to analyze lease rollovers, tenant risk, and NOI growth potential.

- **Examples of Value-Add Projects:**
  - Renovating outdated office buildings to attract higher-paying tenants.
  - Repositioning underutilized retail spaces into mixed-use properties.
  - Optimizing operations for Class B multifamily assets to boost cash flow.

6. **Align Equity Investments with Macro Indicators**
   Macro indicators provide crucial context for equity
   investment decisions:

   - ○ **Interest Rates**: Rising rates affect financing
     costs and cap rates. Use tools like **Bloomberg
     Terminal** to monitor interest rate trends.
   - ○ **Inflation Data**: Tracking CPI or PCE helps
     identify hard assets as inflation hedges.
   - ○ **Bond Market Yields**: Benchmark bond yields
     to evaluate equity return premiums.

7. By integrating macroeconomic insights with
   on-the-ground data, investors can allocate capital
   strategically to mitigate risk and maximize long-term
   value creation.

Practical Example: Strategic Equity Allocation

Imagine a family office managing $30 million in capital
allocation. Using geospatial and demographic data, they
create a diversified equity portfolio:

- **$10 million** into Class A industrial warehouses in **Atlanta** and **Dallas**, targeting logistics hubs benefiting from e-commerce growth.
- **$8 million** into value-added multifamily housing projects in **Phoenix** and **Nashville**, where population growth fuels rental demand.
- **$7 million** into stabilized medical office buildings (MOBs) in **Florida**, capturing long-term demand for healthcare services.
- **$5 million** into mixed-use development opportunities in suburban markets where retail and residential demand intersect.

Each investment targets a specific trend, such as urban migration, healthcare resilience, or logistics demand, while balancing cash flow, appreciation, and risk.

Technology Tools for Equity Management

Sophisticated investors rely on advanced tools to identify, manage, and scale equity investments:

- **CoStar and Reonomy**: Geospatial data for property identification and market analysis.

- **Prophia**: Lease analytics for NOI optimization and risk assessment.
- **Juniper Square**: Centralized platform for investor reporting and joint venture tracking.
- **nBrain.ai**: customize your own proprietary AI-powered intelligence agent that integrates macro indicators, tenant data, and portfolio analytics to drive equity decisions.

These tools ensure data-backed decisions, efficient asset management, and market scalability.

Tying It All Together

Equity-based investments are the backbone of your Hard Asset Empire™, delivering both **growth and stability** through appreciation, cash flow, and direct control. For sophisticated investors and family offices, the key lies in balancing sector and geographic exposure, leveraging advanced tools, and aligning decisions with macroeconomic trends.

The combination of value creation, precision allocation, and strategic diversification ensures that equity investments perform consistently, laying the foundation for generational wealth.

By approaching equity-based investments as both an art and a science—combining hands-on management with data-driven insights—you set the stage for sustained growth. This layer of your financial fortress generates income and acts as a durable hedge against inflation and economic uncertainty.

Debt Instruments: Stability and Predictable Income

While equity-based investments deliver growth and value creation, debt instruments serve as the stabilizing force of your Hard Asset Empire™. Like the steel beams reinforcing the walls of a structure, debt provides stability, resilience, and predictable income that counterbalances the volatility of equity investments. For sophisticated investors, debt-based investments—when carefully structured and strategically integrated—offer **reliable cash flow, risk mitigation, and liquidity management**.

Debt investing does not merely involve straightforward lending; it requires a nuanced approach to terms, collateral assessment, and macroeconomic trends. By combining senior loans, mezzanine financing, and structured opportunities, investors can optimize returns while minimizing exposure to downside risk.

Types of Debt Investments

1. **Senior Debt**
   Senior loans are the bedrock of debt-based investing. These secured loans hold a **first-lien position** on the collateralized asset, making them the safest tier in the capital stack. In the event of default, senior debt holders are first in line to recover their capital through asset liquidation.

   - **Risk Profile:** Low
   - **Returns:** Typically 5-8% annually, depending on the creditworthiness of the borrower and loan duration.

2. **Mezzanine Financing**
   Mezzanine debt is subordinate to senior loans but offers higher interest rates in exchange for moderate risk. It bridges the gap between senior debt and equity, providing borrowers with additional capital while offering lenders enhanced yield opportunities.

Mezzanine financing is particularly useful for value-add projects or acquisitions requiring a blended capital structure.

- ○ **Risk Profile:** Moderate
- ○ **Returns:** 8-14% annually, depending on the risk and structure.

3. **Debt Funds and Syndications**
   For institutional investors and family offices, private debt funds can pool capital and participate in large-scale lending opportunities. These funds often focus on commercial real estate, distressed loans, or structured debt, providing diversified exposure and attractive yields.

   - ○ **Risk Profile:** Varies based on focus and leverage within the fund.
   - ○ **Returns:** Typically 6-12% annually, depending on fund strategy and borrower profile.

Why Debt Instruments Matter

1. **Income Stability**
   Debt instruments deliver **predictable cash flow,**

making them essential to a balanced portfolio. In an uncertain economic environment, fixed-interest payments provide a consistent income stream that can outperform traditional bonds or other fixed-income instruments.

2. **Risk Management**
   Senior debt's **secured nature** reduces exposure, especially during market downturns. By prioritizing loans backed by high-quality collateral—such as stabilized multifamily properties or fully leased commercial assets—you ensure higher capital protection.

3. **Liquidity Preservation**
   Debt investments allow you to **deploy capital strategically** while preserving equity for higher-risk, higher-reward opportunities. By generating steady income, debt positions are a cash flow engine that fuels further acquisitions, renovations, or expansions.

Negotiating Key Debt Terms

Sophisticated investors know that debt structures can make or break a deal. Optimizing terms ensures favorable outcomes and mitigates risk.

1. **Loan-to-Value (LTV)**
   Maintain conservative **LTV ratios** (e.g., 60-70%) to protect your downside. Conservative LTVs provide a cushion if asset values decline and ensure collateral coverage for senior debt holders.

   - **Example:** On a $10 million commercial property, a senior loan with a 65% LTV ratio ($6.5 million loan) preserves a $3.5 million equity cushion to protect lenders in case of market fluctuations.

2. **Interest Rate Structures**
   Lock in favorable interest rates to hedge against rising costs. Consider:

   - **Fixed Rates:** Predictable payments, ideal in a rising rate environment.
   - **Blended Rates:** Combine fixed and variable components to balance stability with flexibility.

3. Use tools like **Bloomberg Terminal** to track the Treasury yield curve and assess market expectations for interest rate movements.

4. **Prepayment Flexibility**
   Ensure the loan terms allow for early repayment without significant penalties. This flexibility provides **agility** to refinance or redeploy capital into higher-yield opportunities.

5. **Recourse vs. Non-Recourse Loans**
   Non-recourse loans limit personal liability to the pledged collateral, shielding your broader portfolio from risk. However, lenders may demand slightly higher interest rates for this concession.

   - **Advanced Tactic:** Pair non-recourse loans with strong equity buffers or cross-collateralization to secure favorable terms.

Data Sources for Identifying Debt Opportunities

Sophisticated investors and institutional funds rely on a variety of data sources to evaluate lending opportunities, assess risk, and identify trends:

1. **Treasury Yield Curve**

   - The yield curve indicates market expectations for future interest rates. A flat or inverted curve can signal economic uncertainty, while a steepening curve points to growth.
   - Use tools like **Bloomberg Terminal** or **Federal Reserve Economic Data (FRED)** to monitor shifts in yields and time debt investments strategically.

2. **CMBS Analytics**

   - Commercial Mortgage-Backed Securities (CMBS) data provides insights into loan performance, default rates, and distressed opportunities.
   - Platforms like **Trepp** offer in-depth analysis of CMBS pools, helping investors identify potential lending opportunities or distressed assets with strong upside potential.

3. **Geospatial and Collateral Data**

    - Tools like **CoStar** and **Reonomy** provide property-level data, tenant occupancy rates, and market trends to evaluate collateral strength.
    - Combining geospatial data with economic indicators helps determine whether specific markets can sustain debt investments.

4. **Macro Indicators**

    - Monitor GDP growth, unemployment rates, and inflation through platforms like **FRED** and **Trading Economics**. Macro indicators provide the broader economic context for lending decisions, especially in uncertain market conditions.

Practical Example: Strategic Debt Placement

A sophisticated investor identifies an opportunity to provide mezzanine financing for a $20 million mixed-use redevelopment project in Denver. The senior lender offers $14 million (70% LTV), leaving a $4 million funding gap for the borrower to complete the project. The investor provides a **$3 million mezzanine loan** secured by a second lien on the property.

- **Loan Terms:**
  - Amount: $3 million
  - Interest Rate: 12% annualized
  - Term: 18 months
  - Collateral Value: $20 million (post-redevelopment)

By underwriting the asset using data from **Trepp** and **Reonomy**, the investor confirms that the post-renovation value will exceed $24 million, creating a strong equity cushion. The loan generates $360,000 in annual interest income while maintaining downside protection through the collateralized second lien.

Debt as the Stabilizing Force

Debt instruments serve as the steel framing that reinforces your financial fortress. They generate **stable, predictable income**, hedge against risk, and provide liquidity to support equity-based growth. By combining senior loans, mezzanine financing, and structured debt funds, investors create a diversified capital strategy capable of thriving in any market condition.

For family offices and institutional funds, the key lies in **precision**:

- Underwrite assets using geospatial data and macroeconomic trends.
- Negotiate favorable terms to align with market cycles and risk profiles.
- Use technology tools like **Trepp**, **Bloomberg Terminal**, and **nBrain.ai** to analyze, monitor, and optimize lending opportunities.

The right balance of debt and equity creates a portfolio that grows and **withstands volatility**, providing a stable foundation for long-term success.

Asset-Based Lending (ABL): Secured Income with Collateralized Downside

While equity-based investments fuel long-term appreciation and debt instruments stabilize cash flow, asset-based lending (ABL) occupies a critical middle ground. It allows sophisticated investors to **leverage tangible assets as collateral to generate high yields with limited downside exposure.** Like the reinforced girders within the steel framework of a fortress, ABL adds strength, flexibility, and risk mitigation to your capital strategy.

Asset-based lending offers a clear path for investors looking to diversify income streams while maintaining capital security. It generates predictable cash flow with returns significantly higher than traditional debt instruments, all while being anchored by valuable collateral. This makes ABL a powerful component in balancing growth, stability, and resilience.

The Mechanics of Asset-Based Lending

At its core, ABL involves issuing loans secured by physical assets or receivables, ensuring lenders have recourse if a borrower defaults. Here's how the process works step by step:

1. **Identify Borrowers**
   ABL typically targets businesses, developers, or investors who require short-term bridge financing, liquidity solutions, or capital for projects such as construction or value-added renovations. Borrowers often include:

   - Real estate developers needing capital to complete a project.

- Businesses requiring liquidity against receivables.
- Investors restructuring loans to unlock asset value.

2. **Evaluate Collateral**

The cornerstone of ABL is **thorough collateral analysis.** Lenders must ensure the pledged asset has sufficient value, liquidity, and stability. Tools like **Trepp** and **CoStar** provide detailed insights into real estate collateral, while **nBrain.ai** centralizes borrower data and automates underwriting processes.

- **Real Estate**: Multifamily, industrial, or commercial properties.
- **Receivables**: Accounts payable from creditworthy businesses.
- **Inventory/Equipment**: Tangible business assets that retain resale value.

3. **Set Loan Structures**

Asset-based loans are typically short-term (6-24 months) and structured to deliver high returns while safeguarding downside risk. Key elements include:

- **LTV Ratios**: Conservative loan-to-value ratios (60-70%) ensure adequate collateral protection.

- Interest Rates: ABL commands higher yields, typically between **8-12% annually**, reflecting the niche nature of the lending.
- Loan Covenants: Define performance benchmarks, asset maintenance requirements, and borrower obligations.

4. **Monitor Performance**

Ongoing oversight of borrower performance and collateral value is critical to ABL success. Platforms like **Juniper Square** streamline loan performance tracking, while tools like **nBrain.ai** provide AI-driven alerts for early signs of borrower default or asset devaluation.

Advanced ABL Strategies for Sophisticated Investors

Sophisticated investors and family offices approach ABL with an eye for efficiency, security, and scalability. Here's how they elevate their strategy:

1. **Bridge Loans for Real Estate Development**

Bridge financing fills funding gaps for developers completing construction or repositioning assets. Investors act as short-term lenders, capturing attractive returns with the property as collateral.

- - **Example**: A $5 million bridge loan to a developer renovating a $7.5 million industrial property generates a 10% annualized return over 12 months. If the borrower defaults, the investor takes control of the asset at a discount.

2. **Receivables-Based Lending**
Businesses with significant accounts receivable offer another opportunity for asset-based lenders. Investors earn returns by advancing funds against outstanding invoices while ensuring repayment through cash flow collections.

- - **Risk Management**: Platforms like **Experian** or **Dun & Bradstreet** assess borrower credit risk, ensuring only quality receivables are financed.

3. **Distressed Asset Recovery**
Savvy investors can acquire underperforming loans at a discount, take control of the collateral, and reposition the asset to extract value. Tools like **Trepp** provide insight into distressed debt pools, identifying underperforming commercial loans ripe for recovery.

- ○ **Example**: Acquiring a distressed $4 million mezzanine loan secured by a $6 million office building allows an investor to foreclose, assume ownership, and reposition the asset for higher occupancy and income.

Technology Tools for Asset-Based Lending

Technology transforms the ABL process, streamlining underwriting, borrower analysis, and risk management:

- **Trepp**: Provides in-depth analytics on commercial real estate performance and distressed debt opportunities.
- **nBrain.ai**: Build a customized enterprise AI agent that centralizes collateral data, borrower credit analysis, and tracking of loan performance. It uses AI-powered insights to predict risk and optimize loan structures.
- **Juniper Square**: A centralized platform for managing loan covenants, investor reporting, and borrower communications.

These tools provide sophisticated investors with **data-driven insights** that reduce risk and maximize efficiency in managing asset-based lending portfolios.

Practical Example: ABL in Action

Imagine a family office with $10 million in liquid capital seeking secured, high-yield opportunities. Instead of deploying all funds into equity-based acquisitions, they allocate $4 million toward ABL. They identify a real estate developer needing a $3 million bridge loan to complete a luxury multifamily renovation project.

- **Loan Terms**:
    - Loan Amount: $3 million
    - LTV: 65% (property appraised at $4.6 million)
    - Interest Rate: 11% annually
    - Term: 18 months

Over the loan term, the family office earns **$495,000 in interest income** while maintaining the property as collateral. If the developer defaults, the office forecloses on the asset and assumes ownership, positioning the property for sale or long-term rental income.

This example highlights the dual benefits of ABL: **attractive yields** and **collateralized downside protection.**

Creating Synergy Between Debt, Equity, and Asset-Based Lending

The key to resilience and growth lies in creating synergy among these three capital components:

1. **Reinvest Cash Flow**
   Interest income from debt and ABL can fund new equity-based acquisitions, creating a self-sustaining cycle of reinvestment and compounding returns.

2. **Leverage Equity for Liquidity**
   Hard assets held within your equity portfolio can serve as collateral for additional loans, providing liquidity for opportunistic investments without requiring asset sales.

3. **Hedge Risk**
   Maintain a diversified allocation to hedge against market cycles.

   For example:

   - **50-60%** in equity-based real estate for long-term growth.
   - **20-30%** in senior debt and mezzanine financing for income stability.

- 10-20% in ABL for secured, high-yield returns.

Summary: Strengthening Resilience with ABL

Asset-based lending (ABL) delivers predictable income while offering secured protection through tangible collateral. It acts as a stabilizing force within your financial fortress, bridging the gap between equity growth and debt stability. For sophisticated investors, ABL provides a unique combination of **high returns, risk mitigation, and liquidity management.**

By integrating advanced tools like **Trepp, nBrain.ai**, and **Juniper Square,** investors can automate underwriting, evaluate borrower performance, and precisely identify opportunities. Combining ABL with equity investments and debt instruments creates a dynamic, resilient portfolio that thrives in all economic conditions.

The synergy between these components ensures every dollar of capital is **efficiently deployed, protected, and optimized**. With this framework in place, your Hard Asset Empire™ is positioned to deliver **growth, stability, and resilience** for future generations.

By strategically balancing equity, debt, and ABL, you lay the groundwork for a robust, dynamic portfolio capable of thriving in any economic environment. Now, let's unlock the immense potential of the coming distressed debt cycle.

In **Chapter 9: The CMBS Debt Bomb — Distressed Opportunities 2025-2028**, we'll explore one of the greatest opportunities in the coming years: commercial mortgage-backed securities (CMBS) maturity. This impending debt crisis will unleash distressed assets, presenting savvy investors with an unprecedented chance to capitalize on discounted opportunities and secure high-value assets for the future.

Endnotes

1. Federal Reserve Economic Data (FRED), "Economic Indicators," https://fred.stlouisfed.org/.
2. Trepp, "Commercial Mortgage-Backed Securities Insights," https://www.trepp.com/.
3. Bloomberg Terminal, "Global Bond and Interest Rate Data," https://www.bloomberg.com/.
4. CoStar, "Real Estate Market Analytics," https://www.costar.com/.
5. Reonomy, "Property and Geospatial Data," https://www.reonomy.com/.
6. nBrain.ai, "AI-Driven Loan Analysis and Risk Management," https://nbrain.ai/.
7. Juniper Square, "Investor and Borrower Management," https://www.junipersquare.com/.
8. Experian, "Business Credit and Risk Insights," https://www.experian.com/.
9. Anderson, Thomas. *The Value of Debt in Building Wealth*. Wiley, 2016.
10. National Association of Realtors, "Commercial Real Estate Outlook," https://www.nar.realtor/.

9

Advanced Strategies– A $2 Trillion Debt Bomb Meets $6.7 Trillion in Dry Powder 2025-2028

The perfect storm for wealth transfer is underway

The commercial real estate (CRE) sector is on the cusp of a historic repricing cycle driven by two colossal forces: the $2 trillion in maturing CMBS (Commercial Mortgage-Backed Securities) debt coming due between 2025 and 2028, and a staggering $6.7 trillion parked in money market funds awaiting deployment. This confluence creates one of the greatest wealth transfer opportunities of the 21st century for investors with liquidity, strategic insight, and disciplined use of leverage.

This chapter outlines how sophisticated investors can capitalize on distressed and repriced assets by understanding the dynamics of the maturing debt crisis, deploying cash efficiently, and executing advanced acquisition strategies. It also underscores critical lessons on leverage: while it can amplify wealth-building, it must be used surgically during times of volatility.

Understanding the $2 Trillion CMBS Debt Bomb

The maturity wall of CMBS loans is unprecedented. Many of these loans, originated during the low-interest rate years of 2012-2021, are now reaching maturity in an environment where borrowing costs have doubled or even tripled.

1. Refinancing Risk and NOI Pressures

Properties financed with loans at 3-4% interest rates are now being refinanced at rates closer to 7-9%. The implications are severe:

- **Higher Debt Service:** Many properties no longer generate enough Net Operating Income (NOI) to support the new debt payments.

- **Declining Values:** Elevated cap rates due to higher interest rates are compressing property valuations.
- **Equity Erosion:** Owners facing cash flow deficits may lose their equity or be forced to offload properties at distressed prices.

For example, a $50 million multifamily property with $35 million of debt at a 3% interest rate had a $1.05 million annual debt service. Refinancing the same loan at 7% would increase debt service to $2.45 million annually, effectively wiping out the property's cash flow unless NOI increases significantly.

2. The Lending Market Tightens

Banks and traditional lenders, facing balance sheet constraints and regulatory scrutiny, are pulling back from CRE lending. This tightening means fewer refinancing options and lower Loan-to-Value (LTV) ratios, leaving many borrowers without lifelines.

Advanced Insight: Investors with liquidity and access to bridge financing can step in to acquire these assets at deep discounts or negotiate favorable terms with distressed sellers.

The $6.7 Trillion Money Market Opportunity

As of December 2024, $6.7 trillion is sitting idle in U.S. money market funds, reflecting investor caution and a desire for safety in a high-rate environment. This unprecedented pool of capital includes:

- Government Funds: $5.56 trillion (institutional and retail).
- Prime Funds: $1.07 trillion.
- Tax-Exempt Funds: $137 billion.

This liquidity, while earning modest yields of 4-5%, represents a massive "dry powder" reserve poised to flow into undervalued assets as opportunities arise. Investors who combine their liquidity with disciplined use of debt can strategically redeploy this capital for outsized returns.

The Advanced Strategy: Acquiring Distressed CRE in the Great Repricing

1. Focus on Cash-Flowing Assets at Discounted Prices

With rising interest rates and higher debt service costs forcing owners to sell, many CRE assets, especially multifamily and office properties, will be available at substantial discounts. Key steps include:

- **Identify Distressed Sellers:** Look for properties nearing loan maturity where owners cannot refinance. Tools like Trepp and CoStar provide CMBS maturity data and identify at-risk loans.
- **Evaluate Stabilized NOI:** Even if a property's current NOI is depressed, focus on its long-term stabilization potential post-acquisition.
- **Structure Favorable Financing:** Use bridge loans or private financing to acquire assets, and reposition them for long-term stabilization and refinancing at better terms.

2. Target Markets with Resilient Demographics

Not all markets will face the same pressures. Target regions with robust fundamentals, including:

- Population Growth: Markets like Texas, Florida, and Arizona are seeing rapid population influxes, sustaining multifamily demand.
- Resilient Tenant Demand: In office and retail, focus on medical office buildings (MOBs), industrial warehouses, and essential services, where cash flow is resilient.

Example: A distressed multifamily asset in Austin, originally valued at $30 million, is forced into a sale at $22 million due to loan maturity. With moderate NOI improvements and favorable financing, an investor can achieve 20-30% equity returns within 24-36 months.

Leverage: Amplifying Returns Without Overextending

Leverage remains a critical tool for investors seeking to capitalize on the Great Repricing, but it must be wielded carefully. Overleveraging, especially in a high-rate environment, can turn opportunities into financial traps.

Proper Use of Leverage

- **Conservative LTV Ratios:** Aim for LTVs of 65-70%, ensuring equity cushions during economic volatility.
- **Fixed-Rate Debt:** Lock in fixed financing where possible to hedge against future rate increases.
- **Stress Test Investments:** Analyze worst-case scenarios, including higher vacancies, lower NOI, or further rate hikes, to ensure assets remain solvent.

Blackstone's 2008 Lessons Revisited

During the 2008 financial crisis, savvy investors like Blackstone capitalized on distressed CRE assets, acquiring properties at discounts as high as 40-50%. They understood two critical lessons:

1. **Liquidity is Power**: Those with access to capital could step in when others were sidelined by financial strain.
2. **Long-Term Vision:** The assets acquired during the crisis appreciated significantly as markets stabilized, generating massive returns.

The 2025-2028 repricing cycle represents a similar opportunity. Institutional investors, family offices, and strategic funds must position themselves now to deploy capital at scale.

Action Plan: Capitalizing on the Great Repricing

Step 1: Build Liquidity and Partnerships

- Accumulate cash reserves to capitalize on distressed opportunities.
- Partner with private lenders, bridge loan providers, and capital partners to expand buying power.

Step 2: Use Technology to Find Opportunities

- Trepp: Monitor CMBS maturities and distressed loans.

- CoStar: Identify undervalued properties and market trends.
- nBrain.ai: Use AI to centralize data and uncover actionable opportunities.

Step 3: Negotiate from a Position of Strength

- Target loan maturities and distressed sellers, leveraging liquidity to negotiate deep discounts.
- Pursue seller financing or assume existing loans to minimize refinancing risk.

Step 4: Implement a Long-Term Value Strategy

- Acquire assets with strong NOI potential in growth markets.
- Reposition or redevelop properties to maximize income and stabilize for future refinancing.

Summary: A Once-in-a-Generation Opportunity

The collision of $2 trillion in maturing CMBS debt and $6.7 trillion in money market reserves creates an unparalleled opportunity for investors to capitalize on the Great Repricing of 2025-2028. By targeting distressed assets, deploying capital strategically, and leveraging conservatively, savvy investors can unlock massive discounts, stabilize high-value properties, and drive outsized returns.

History favors the prepared. As the market shifts, those with liquidity, insight, and discipline will transform this crisis into a wealth-building triumph.

Endnotes

1. Trepp, "CMBS Maturity Outlook 2024–2028," https://www.trepp.com.
2. CoStar, "U.S. Commercial Real Estate Debt Trends," https://www.costar.com.
3. Investment Company Institute, "Money Market Fund Assets," December 2024.
4. Marcus & Millichap, "CRE Trends and Opportunities 2025," https://www.marcusmillichap.com.
5. Deloitte, "Commercial Real Estate and Debt Strategies," https://www2.deloitte.com.
6. Urban Land Institute, *Emerging Trends in Real Estate 2024*, https://uli.org/reports.
7. Federal Reserve Bank of St. Louis, "Economic Indicators and Interest Rate Trends," https://fred.stlouisfed.org.
8. JPMorgan Insights, "CMBS Debt Challenges in a High-Rate Environment," 2024.
9. Zais Group, "CRE Refinancing Risks and Opportunities," https://zaisgroup.com.
10. Multihousing News, "Multifamily Market Challenges and Distressed Opportunities," December 2024.
11. Blackstone Insights, "Lessons Learned from the 2008 Crisis: Acquiring Distressed Assets," 2023.
12. Trepp, "Impact of Higher Interest Rates on CRE Asset Pricing," https://www.trepp.com.
13. Deloitte Insights, "Leverage Strategies for Commercial Real Estate Investors," 2024.
14. Nareit, "REIT Trends and Cap Rate Forecasts," https://www.nareit.com.
15. Investment Company Institute, "Trends in Money Market Funds and Liquidity Deployment," December 2024.
16. Sortis Blog, "Interest Rate Impact on Debt Markets," https://sortis.com/blog.
17. Bloomberg, "The Great Repricing: $2 Trillion in CMBS Debt Bomb," November 2024.

18. Marcus & Millichap, "Regional Disruptions and Florida's Condo Cliff," December 2024.
19. Federal Reserve Insights, "Liquidity Trends and Real Estate Capital Allocation," 2024
20. CoStar Analytics, "Distressed Opportunities and Market Forecast," https://www.costar.com.

10

The Future of Bitcoin - Deflationary Capital in an Inflationary World

One of the most revolutionary aspects of Bitcoin is its ability to serve as deflationary collateral — a concept fundamentally different from traditional forms of collateral like real estate or fiat-based assets. By borrowing against Bitcoin, investors can unlock capital at a fraction of the risk required by inflationary systems while maintaining exposure to Bitcoin's upside potential.

In a world where fiat currencies continually lose purchasing power due to inflation, Bitcoin's fixed supply (21 million) ensures its long-term value appreciates against fiat assets. This dynamic creates asymmetric opportunities for investors who leverage Bitcoin as collateral to borrow inflationary fiat, which can then be used to acquire real estate, equities, or other cash-flowing assets.

Bitcoin, unlike traditional assets, reduces the risk of over-leveraging because:

1. Collateral Efficiency: Bitcoin appreciates over time, requiring less collateral to borrow the same amount of fiat.
2. Deflationary Nature: Borrowers benefit from Bitcoin's scarcity and increasing value while repaying loans in devalued fiat currency.
3. Bank Disintermediation: Bitcoin holders can access liquidity without relying on banks, intermediaries, or credit markets that tighten during economic downturns.

Case Study: Real Estate with Bitcoin Collateral vs Fiat

Let's revisit a real estate transaction to demonstrate Bitcoin's role as efficient collateral in an inflationary environment. The following example was a real transaction in USD values in Scottsdale, Arizona (figure 1.0). This chart shows the amount of Bitcoin or alternative Fiat currencies it would have taken to purchase or collateralize the acquisition.

Date	USD	YEN	EUROS	BITCOIN
June 3, 2017 (Purchase)	$432,900	¥48,284,460	€385,281	฿173.16
January 2, 2022 (Sale)	$835,000	¥96,225,000	€737,710	฿17.60

Figure 1.0 Source: Wealth Matters 3.0 Substack
(https://www.wealthmatterstome.com/p/bitcoin-hits-100k-and-why-this-all)

The Analysis

1. Initial Purchase in 2017:
   - The property was purchased for $432,900, requiring ₱173.16 as collateral at the time. Bitcoin's price in 2017 was significantly lower, which meant more Bitcoin was required to collateralize the purchase.
2. Sale in 2022:
   - By January 2, 2022, the property appreciated to $835,000—almost double its original value in fiat terms when it closed the sale at $55,000 over asking due to five all-cash offers competing.
   - However, Bitcoin had undergone a dramatic appreciation, reducing the amount of Bitcoin needed for the same capital. The collateral required for this transaction dropped to ₱17.60,

a 90% reduction in Bitcoin collateral to secure nearly double the fiat value.

A Modern Theoretical Example: Bitcoin at $100,000 to $200,000

Now, let's bring this concept into 2024's market dynamics. As of the writing of this chapter, Bitcoin has recently eclipsed the $100,000 milestone and held steady above it for a few weeks. Imagine Bitcoin is valued at $100,000 when the borrowing occurs:

- An investor borrows $1 million in fiat against ₿10 at $100,000 per Bitcoin.
- A year later, Bitcoin appreciates to $200,000 per coin, effectively doubling the value of the investor's Bitcoin collateral. The original $1 million loan now represents just 50% Loan-to-Value (LTV), reducing the risk profile of the loan dramatically.

Outcome:

- The investor secures a valuable real estate asset using Bitcoin as collateral.
- As Bitcoin appreciates, the investor's effective collateral requirement drops, further reducing risk.

- The loan is repaid with devalued fiat currency, effectively arbitraging the difference between Bitcoin's deflationary nature and fiat's inflation-driven purchasing power.
- The naysayers tend to focus on the volatility index and historical cyclical pullbacks in Bitcoin, and although this is not without data or surface level merit the reality is that as the figure 1.1 below shows Bitcoin has outperformed every other asset class in the last four years by orders of magnitude, and unless the governments of the world decide suddenly they will no longer be printing money at the rate of trillions at a time, this arbitrage has merely just begun.

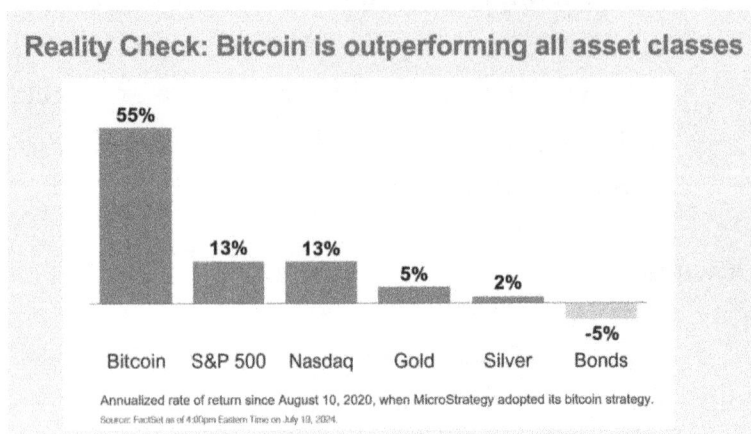

Reality Check: Bitcoin is outperforming all asset classes

Bitcoin	S&P 500	Nasdaq	Gold	Silver	Bonds
55%	13%	13%	5%	2%	-5%

Annualized rate of return since August 10, 2020, when MicroStrategy adopted its bitcoin strategy.
Source: FactSet as of 4:00pm Eastern Time on July 19, 2024.

Figure 1.1 Source: Michael Saylor Keynote at Cantor
(https://www.youtube.com/watch?v=OA3DGM0vgtM)

Borrowing Against Bitcoin: Alternative Capital During Hard Times

Banks and financial institutions tighten lending standards in traditional economic downturns, reducing liquidity for businesses and investors. This scenario leaves many asset holders "cash poor" despite owning valuable assets. Bitcoin, however, changes the rules of the game:

1. **Collateral-Based Liquidity**: Bitcoin-backed loans enable investors to borrow fiat without selling their Bitcoin. Platforms like *Unchained Capital*, *Ledn*, and *BlockFi* offer Bitcoin-backed loans at competitive interest rates, bypassing traditional lenders entirely.

2. **Deflationary Leverage**: Borrowing against Bitcoin allows investors to capitalize on fiat liquidity to purchase real-world assets. As fiat depreciates and Bitcoin appreciates, the borrower repays the loan with devalued dollars while retaining ownership of the hard asset.

3. **Risk Mitigation**: Unlike banks, Bitcoin loans are secured directly by the asset (Bitcoin), reducing

systemic counterparty risks. If markets falter, Bitcoin-backed borrowers maintain flexibility.

Strategic Opportunity for Real Estate Investors

Let's explore the updated concept of using Bitcoin-backed loans to purchase real estate during an inflationary cycle:

- An investor borrows $1 million in fiat against ₱10 when Bitcoin costs $100,000.
- The investor uses the borrowed capital to acquire a rental property generating annual cash flow.
- Over time, Bitcoin appreciates to $200,000 per coin, reducing the loan-to-value (LTV) ratio to 25%. Simultaneously, the rental property appreciates with inflation while providing ongoing cash flow.
- The investor repays the loan with devalued fiat, effectively arbitraging the difference between Bitcoin's deflationary nature and the inflation-driven fiat market.

This strategy creates a self-reinforcing cycle: Bitcoin serves as collateral for real estate acquisition, the acquired property generates cash flow to pay down fiat loans, and Bitcoin continues to appreciate, further reducing collateral risk. It's a trifecta of wealth creation: cash flow, asset appreciation, and deflationary leverage.

Open Source Bitcoin 24 Model for 21-year Projection Analysis:

Bitcoin24 is designed to simulate 21-year outcomes of various Bitcoin strategies tailored for individuals, corporations, institutions, and nation-states. Users can input their assumptions or adjust the model to explore different scenarios. Saving the file will automatically update the scenario comparison charts in the micro models' bottom section.

Bitcoin24 does not model Bitcoin's volatility, as its volatility profile has evolved and will continue to do so in the future. This simplified model is intended to show possible long-term outcomes of adopting a Bitcoin standard. Visit it by typing in this URL to your browser, and give it to your financial analyst and team to help you create your assumptions and strategy.

Copy this into your favorite web browser to create your models. https://github.com/bitcoin-model/bitcoin_model
The Model's Original Authors/Contributors include:
- Michael J. Saylor
- Shirish Jajodia
- Chaitanya Jain (CJ)

- ***Personal Referral Note:*** *If you are interested in a bespoke private-client brokerage for Bitcoin lending at 65% LTV with great terms and five (5) day turnarounds from the account setup and application process you should look into Secure Digital Markets at* https://www.sdm.co *and ask for James Godfrey (Principal /Lending Desk lead) and tell them you are part of the Hard Asset Empire™ Builder family. They can also help you set up an Over-the-Counter (OTC) bespoke account with industry low transaction fees (approximately 20bps above spot) and bespoke covered-call option strategies for their high net worth clients. Minimum orders on the OTC side are around $500,000 and no limit, and the average BTC loan amount floor is around $250,000 into the $10s of millions.*

Disintermediating Banks: Bitcoin Treasury Advantage

By leveraging Bitcoin as a reserve and borrowing asset, sophisticated investors and family offices can bypass traditional capital markets that often restrict liquidity during economic downturns. Bitcoin-backed loans create a parallel financial system that:

- Reduces reliance on credit-dependent banks.
- Provides immediate liquidity for asset acquisition.
- Maintains Bitcoin exposure while unlocking fiat capital.

Key Benefits:

1. Capital Efficiency: Bitcoin holders can borrow fiat at a fraction of traditional collateral requirements.
2. Asset Retention: Unlike traditional sales, Bitcoin-backed borrowing avoids triggering taxable events or forfeiting upside potential.
3. Inflation Arbitrage: As inflation increases, the value of hard assets (real estate, commodities), borrowers repay loans with increasingly devalued currency.

Final Thoughts on Bitcoin:

Bitcoin's role as a deflationary collateral asset represents a paradigm shift in capital management. By borrowing against Bitcoin, investors can:

- Acquire hard assets like real estate using inflationary dollars.

- Multiply wealth while preserving Bitcoin's long-term appreciation potential.
- Disintermediate banks during periods of liquidity crunches and economic uncertainty.

The real estate example demonstrates the transformative power of Bitcoin: ₱10 at $100,000 could secure $1 million in fiat capital today. At the same time, Bitcoin's appreciation to $200,000 per coin reduces the loan-to-value ratio to 25%, further securing the investor's position. This strategy compounds wealth and protects capital in an environment where inflation erodes the purchasing power of fiat currencies.

As we move into a world where Bitcoin is increasingly recognized as digital capital, sophisticated investors will use it as a cornerstone for hybrid cash flow management and treasury reserve strategies. By doing so, they will position their portfolios to thrive during inflationary cycles, economic downturns, and systemic disruptions.

Food for thought: Imagine holding ₱10 today as collateral and acquiring assets worth millions tomorrow, all while fiat loses its grip and Bitcoin compounds in value. This isn't just the future of finance—it's the beginning of a new era for capital preservation and generational wealth creation.

Bitcoin as a Hybrid Cash Flow and Treasury Reserve Strategy

So that is one novel and future-forward advanced strategy for how you could leverage Bitcoin as the ultimate collateral to accumulate inflationary, cash-flow generating, real estate assets with arbitrage, but now let's discuss a hybrid cash flow management treasury reserve strategy inspired by the bold and controversial moves of Microstrategy's Michael Saylor. First, let's make sure we do a quick history lesson on the history of (sound) hard money versus fiat currency.

The History of Hard Money vs. Fiat Currency

To understand the revolutionary role of Bitcoin in financial capital management, we need to begin with the foundational principles of "hard money" (sound money) and fiat currency. Hard money has historically been a *scarce, durable, and decentralized medium of value*—gold being its most iconic example. Sound money maintains purchasing power over time, acting as a bulwark against inflation and financial entropy.

On the other hand, Fiat currencies emerged as convenient tools for trade and growth but became untethered from real-world scarcity after the abandonment of the gold standard in 1971. The consequences have been severe: monetary inflation, asset price bubbles, and a decline in purchasing power, all exacerbated by excessive money printing and political intervention.

Figure 1.2 clearly illustrates how inflation erodes purchasing power. Over the last 14 years, very few asset classes have outpaced monetary inflation (as high as 15%), while Bitcoin delivered unparalleled returns of 60% annualized.

Value of a U.S. Dollar
Compared to a 1913 dollar

In a world where fiat currencies act as "melting ice cubes," the need for a new reserve asset is undeniable. As a form of digital capital and sound money, Bitcoin solves this problem.

The Economic Problem: Outpacing Inflation and Cost of Capital

The economic challenge is clear: most asset classes fail to outperform inflation, let alone the rising cost of capital. This creates a structural issue for institutions, corporations, and investors alike.

- **Inflationary Erosion**: Fiat-based cash reserves lose value at a rate of 10-15% annually. Holding $100 billion in US treasuries effectively costs shareholders $10-15 billion annually in purchasing power.
- **The Cost of Capital**: Companies that cannot consistently deliver 15% annualized returns are punished by institutional investors, leading to reduced liquidity and long-term decline.
- **Debt Dependency**: Corporate strategies relying on leverage, stock buybacks, or dividend payouts create unsustainable growth models.

Michael Saylor describes this as a "Type 1 diabetic" problem—companies must constantly inject liquidity into a system that fundamentally loses value.

The Solution: Bitcoin is a treasury reserve asset that compounds value over time. It's uncorrelated, high-yield performance shields against inflation while delivering generational returns. Over the past 14 years Bitcoin's annualized performance (60%) outstrips every other asset class, including equities, real estate, and gold.

The Hard Asset Empire™ Hybrid: Bitcoin as a CRE Cash Flow Treasury Reserve Strategy

Balancing a mix of equity, debt, and Bitcoin as a hybrid treasury reserve strategy for sophisticated investors, family offices, and institutional funds unlocks unprecedented efficiency and growth potential. By integrating Bitcoin into a diversified capital allocation model, you create three distinct advantages:

1. **Inflation Hedge**: Bitcoin preserves capital over long time horizons, unlike fiat reserves or underperforming bonds.
2. **Yield Amplification**: Incorporating Bitcoin-based strategies, like MicroStrategy's model, allows for leveraged performance with reduced counterparty risk.
3. **Generational Preservation**: Bitcoin operates as a "thousand-year asset," a term Michael Saylor coined to describe its immutable, global, and secure nature.

Building a Treasury Reserve Blueprint

The Hard Asset Empire™ Hybrid Bitcoin Treasury Strategy focuses on four core principles:

1. Capital Allocation Model

Sophisticated investors use data-driven models to allocate capital between Bitcoin, hard assets, and cash-flowing instruments.

- Equities and Hard Assets (50-60%): Real estate, infrastructure, and commercial properties provide cash flow and stability.
- Debt Instruments (20-30%): Senior loans, bonds, and private credit generate predictable yields.
- Bitcoin Reserve (10-20%): As a treasury reserve, Bitcoin delivers asymmetric returns and inflation-proof preservation.

Case Study: MicroStrategy implemented a similar model by issuing bonds to purchase Bitcoin, resulting in returns that outperformed the S&P 500.

2. Data Sources for Bitcoin-Driven Treasury Models

Institutional-grade capital allocation relies on a combination of macroeconomic indicators and real-time financial data:

- Geospatial and Demographic Data: Tools like *CoStar* and *Reonomy* identify regions for asset growth.
- Macroeconomic Indicators: *FRED* and *Treasury Yield Curve* data inform interest rate and monetary policy decisions.
- Bitcoin Analytics: Platforms like *Glassnode* and *nBrain.ai* offer insights into Bitcoin's on-chain activity, volatility, and long-term trends.

3. Structured Leverage and Fixed-Income Strategies

A Bitcoin-backed leverage strategy combines elements of fixed-income performance with digital asset upside:

- Issue Low-Cost Bonds: Raise capital for your CRE fund at fixed interest rates and deploy funds into Bitcoin while you borrow fiat to acquire cash-flowing assets.
- Sell Volatility: Use covered call options or structured notes to generate yields while retaining Bitcoin exposure.

- Secure Downside: Maintain collateralized positions with conservative Loan-to-Value (LTV) ratios, ensuring risk-adjusted performance.

Practical Example: A $50 million family office allocates 20% of its portfolio into Bitcoin-backed CRE fund bonds. By leveraging Bitcoin as collateral, the office secures 8-10% fixed yields while maintaining exposure to Bitcoin's price appreciation and having a downside protection of the preferred returns on the cash-flowing real estate collateral.

Resilient Plan: Bitcoin as a Counterparty-Free Asset

One of Bitcoin's most compelling features is its ability to function as a "counterparty-free" asset. Unlike fiat, bonds, or equities, Bitcoin:

- Cannot be devalued by governments or corporations.
- Is immune to credit risk, cultural shifts, or political volatility.
- Operates independently of any centralized control.

This orthogonal quality positions Bitcoin as the "Holy Grail" of capital preservation for global investors. Bitcoin remains uncorrelated to traditional markets while delivering superior Sharpe ratios.

Example: If a sovereign wealth fund, pension fund, insurance company, or family office holds $1 billion in treasuries, inflation erodes its purchasing power by 10% annually. Reallocating 10% into Bitcoin through a CRE Fund's Bitcoin Bond not only hedges against inflation but compounds returns exponentially with double the hard-asset protection (real estate cash flows and appreciation plus the Bitcoin exposure) all without the need to set up cold storage wallets or institutional custody. They already know how to own mezzanine or preferred equity and debt inside of CRE fund limited partnerships.

The Long-Term Outlook: Bitcoin as a Generational Asset

Michael Saylor argues that Bitcoin's true utility lies in its ability to serve as digital capital—free from physical and financial risk. It solves a multi-trillion-dollar problem: the preservation of generational wealth.

Bitcoin vs. Traditional Hard Assets

While real estate, gold, and bonds remain dominant stores of value, they are not without challenges:

- Real Estate: Maintenance costs, taxation, and regional risks.
- Gold: Physical storage, limited portability, and lack of yield.
- Bonds: Rising interest rates and declining real returns.

In contrast, Bitcoin provides:

- Portability: Transferable across borders instantly and securely.
- Durability: Immune to decay, natural disasters, and physical entropy.
- Scalability: Accessible to any investor, anywhere, at any scale.

Clipped from Saylor's keynote presentation Figure 1.3 shows how global wealth is distributed across asset classes today. Figure 1.4 forecasts a dramatic shift toward Bitcoin by 2045, with its market cap growing to $280 trillion.

Figure 1.3

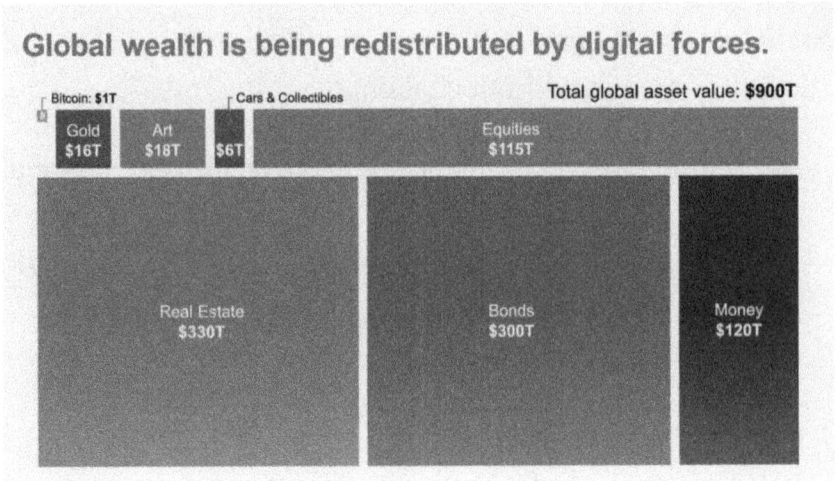

Global wealth is being redistributed by digital forces.

Bitcoin: $1T
Cars & Collectibles
Total global asset value: $900T
Gold $16T
Art $18T
$6T
Equities $115T
Real Estate $330T
Bonds $300T
Money $120T

Figure 1.4

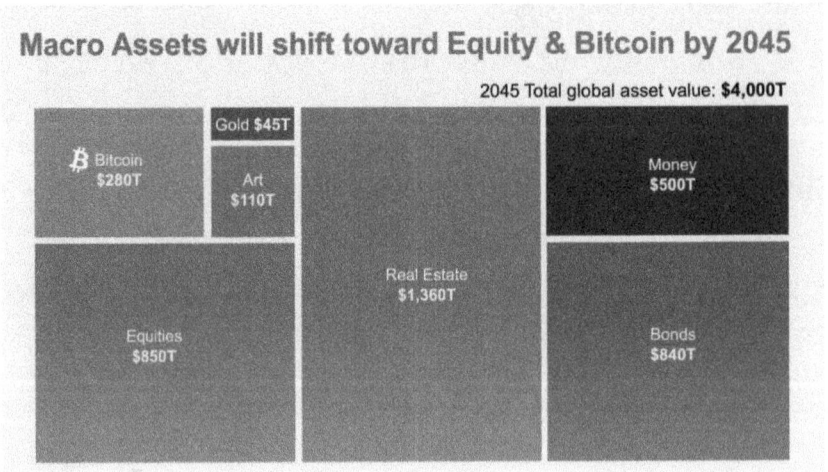

Macro Assets will shift toward Equity & Bitcoin by 2045

2045 Total global asset value: $4,000T
Bitcoin $280T
Gold $45T
Art $110T
Money $500T
Equities $850T
Real Estate $1,360T
Bonds $840T

Summary: Reinventing Capital Allocation with Bitcoin

Integrating Bitcoin into a hybrid treasury reserve strategy is not just a hedge—it's a transformative approach to wealth management. For family offices, institutional investors, and sophisticated funds, Bitcoin provides a scalable, resilient, and asymmetric solution to the inflationary and capital erosion problems caused by fiat currencies.

By balancing hard assets, debt instruments, and Bitcoin:

- You stabilize cash flow with traditional assets.
- You amplify returns with Bitcoin-backed leverage strategies.
- You preserve generational wealth with counterparty-free digital capital.

The result is a financial fortress built for the 21st century that thrives in volatility, preserves value across generations, and positions your Hard Asset Empire™ for exponential growth.

In the final chapter, we'll explore one of the most tried and true gifts that keep giving in the Alliance portfolio, and how you can take advantage of the advanced strategies for owning **Medical Office and Veterinary Office buildings** as the human body and pets never go out of style.

Endnotes

1. Saylor, Michael. *Bitcoin Treasury Strategy*, MicroStrategy World, 2024.
2. Fidelity Investments, "Bitcoin as a Portfolio Diversifier: Sharpe Ratios and Correlation Trends," 2024.
3. Trepp, "CMBS Market Outlook: Maturities and Risk Assessment," 2024.
4. Glassnode, "On-Chain Bitcoin Performance Metrics," 2024.
5. Federal Reserve Economic Data (FRED), "US Monetary Inflation Trends," 2024.
6. Jesse Myers, *Global Wealth Distribution and Bitcoin's Role*, 2024.
7. BlackRock, "Spot Bitcoin ETF Adoption and Capital Allocation Trends," 2024.

11

Advanced Strategies: Medical Office Buildings - The Cash Flow Gift Horse That Keeps on Giving

In the world of commercial real estate, cash flow reigns supreme. Without consistent and predictable income, even the most impressive property can crumble under the weight of debt obligations, operational expenses, and market volatility. **Medical Office Buildings (MOBs)** are unique in their ability to offer a steady income stream due to recession-resilient tenants, long-term lease structures, and a growing demand for healthcare services.

Alliance has been at the forefront of MOB investments for two decades, recognizing their value long before they became a mainstream asset class. As the next decade unfolds, demographic trends, societal shifts, and the rising demand for healthcare and veterinary services will solidify MOBs as the ultimate cash flow asset. This gift horse keeps on giving.

Why Medical Office Buildings Are Cash Flow Titans

1. A Demographic Goldmine

Demographic shifts are the cornerstone of MOB demand. As the population ages, the need for accessible, outpatient care and specialized services continues to grow.

- Baby Boomers: Over 10,000 baby boomers turn 65 daily in the United States, with life expectancy stretching well into the 80s and beyond. The baby boomer generation is set to demand more frequent healthcare visits, ranging from routine care to specialized treatment for age-related conditions like cardiology, orthopedics, and oncology. By 2030, more than 73 million Americans will be over the age of 65, accounting for 20% of the U.S. population.
- DINKs and DINKWADs: The rise of *Dual Income, No Kids* (DINK) households, and their playful subset, *Dual Income, No Kids With A Dog* (DINKWADs), brings a new wave of economic activity. These households prioritize health and wellness, spending heavily on preventative care, elective procedures, and veterinary services.

According to the American Pet Products Association, pet-related healthcare spending exceeded $36 billion in 2023 and is projected to grow annually.

These two demographics alone—aging boomers and health-conscious dual-income earners—drive demand for medical and veterinary office spaces, making MOBs an asset class poised for unparalleled resilience.

2. Recession-Resilient Tenants

Medical office tenants provide non-discretionary services—people need healthcare whether the economy is expanding or contracting. Unlike traditional office spaces, which are increasingly vacant due to remote work trends, MOBs enjoy:

- **Low Turnover Rates:** Relocating becomes prohibitively expensive once a tenant invests in medical infrastructure (like diagnostic equipment or specialized facilities).
- **Long-Term Leases:** Most MOB leases run for 7 to 15 years, with built-in rent escalations, providing landlords with a steady, inflation-hedged income.
- **Tenant Stability:** Healthcare tenants, from large physician groups to outpatient clinics, enjoy reliable

insurance reimbursements and predictable revenue streams, translating into consistent rent payments.

Advanced Strategies for MOB Investment Success

1. Identify High-Demand Submarkets

The key to unlocking MOB success lies in targeting markets with favorable demographic and economic trends:

- Suburban Growth Hubs: Suburban and secondary markets are witnessing population surges as more people seek affordable living while retaining access to healthcare.
- Healthcare Hubs: Focus on MOBs near hospitals, outpatient facilities, and research centers where patient demand is highest.
- DINK and Pet-Friendly Regions: Urban and suburban markets with affluent DINK and DINKWAD populations have rising demand for elective medical and veterinary services.

Tools to Leverage:

- CoStar Analytics: Market data for identifying high-demand locations.

- Esri ArcGIS: Geospatial tools to analyze population growth and healthcare infrastructure gaps.
- Marcus & Millichap Healthcare Reports: Regional breakdowns of MOB performance trends.

---

2. Prioritize Value-Add Opportunities

Medical office buildings are often older properties needing modernization to meet the evolving needs of healthcare providers and patients. Value-add strategies include:

- Upgrading Infrastructure: Install advanced HVAC systems, diagnostic equipment-ready power grids, and modern interiors.
- Telemedicine Integration: Equip spaces with telehealth capabilities, including high-speed internet and virtual consultation rooms.
- Sustainability Improvements: Implement energy-efficient upgrades like LED lighting and solar panels to reduce operating costs and attract environmentally conscious tenants.

---

3. Structure Leases to Maximize Cash Flow

Lease terms are the foundation of MOB profitability. To ensure predictable, long-term cash flow:

- Triple-Net (NNN) Leases: Pass operating expenses like property taxes, insurance, and maintenance onto tenants.
- Annual Rent Escalations: Tie rent increases to inflation or fixed annual percentages (e.g., 2–3%).
- Tenant Improvement (TI) Packages: Offer upfront incentives to attract high-quality tenants, ensuring they stay long-term.

By locking in strong lease terms and partnering with reliable healthcare tenants, MOB landlords create a cash flow machine capable of weathering any market condition.

---

4. Hedge Inflation and Maximize Financing

In an inflationary environment, MOBs outperform other asset classes due to their built-in resilience:

- Inflation-Protected Leases: Rent escalations indexed to the Consumer Price Index (CPI) protect against rising costs.

- Fixed-Rate Financing: Locking in favorable, long-term debt terms ensures predictable cash flow.
- Reinvestment Opportunities: Use cash flow from MOBs to acquire additional assets or diversify into asset-based lending for secured income.

Example: A $5 million suburban MOB acquired with a fixed-rate loan, a tenant mix of primary care providers, and a veterinary clinic can generate 8–10% annualized cash flow, even in rising-rate environments.

Alliance Pioneered MOBs: Lessons From the Past, Tools for the Future

The sector was far from obvious when Alliance entered the MOB market over 20 years ago. At the time, investors favored multifamily and retail, neglecting the demographic certainty underpinning MOB demand. By recognizing the needs of aging boomers and healthcare innovation trends, Alliance positioned itself ahead of the curve.

Key lessons for today's investors include:

- Early Adoption Wins: Identifying asset classes driven by demographic inevitability gives investors a long runway for growth.
- Tenant Relationships Are Assets: MOBs thrive on long-term partnerships with healthcare providers. Prioritizing tenant satisfaction ensures renewals and NOI growth.
- Cash Flow Is King: MOBs provide stable income in volatile markets, insulating portfolios from economic shocks.

The MOB Advantage and Why It Will Endure

Medical office buildings represent the perfect storm of resilience, cash flow, and demographic demand. As baby boomers age and DINK/DINKWAD populations prioritize health and wellness, MOBs will only increase in importance as a core real estate asset class.

By focusing on value-add opportunities, strategic leasing, and inflation-proof financing, investors can unlock the full potential of MOBs—creating stable, compounding cash flow for decades to come.

MOBs are not a passing trend. They are an evergreen opportunity, cementing themselves as the cash flow gift horse that keeps giving, no matter the economic climate.

As you finish your journey through the **Hard Asset Empire™ blueprint**, you must reflect on the deeper principles that drive enduring success.

Building wealth in hard assets is about more than numbers on a spreadsheet—it's about vision, resilience, and leadership. Success comes from identifying opportunities and leading teams, making tough decisions, and cultivating the patience to see strategies through.

In the **Afterword**, we'll explore:

- **Leadership Principles**: The mindset and discipline required to navigate uncertainty and build an enduring legacy.
- **Building High-Performing Teams:** Real estate is a team sport. Surround yourself with the right talent—partners, property managers, and advisors—to execute at scale.
- **Your Ultimate Weapon:** When hard times hit, your ability to adapt, stay focused, and find creative solutions will determine your success.

This final chapter is a personal reflection and mutual call to action to ensure that no matter how volatile the world becomes, you remain equipped to thrive, adapt, and leave a lasting legacy, and I continue to put leading by the example above all else. Your journey in this book is almost over, but your renewed power to systematically build your Hard Asset Empire™ alongside me as I continue building mine is just beginning.

Afterword

The Ultimate Weapon for Building Your Hard Asset Empire Is Your Mind!

We have reached the end of our initial journey in this book, but our true journey together is just beginning and I am grateful to be a part of your story as you use these lessons to enrich your family for generations to come. Remember we are all blessed with unlimited potential, but finite and unknown amounts of time on this planet, so exercising our minds and will to unleash as much of our potential as possible is the race we all run.

The ultimate weapon for building your Hard Asset Empire™ and generational wealth blueprint is **your leadership, mindset, and the culture of loyalty within your ecosystem**. Assets are the tools, blueprints, and strategies are the playbooks, **but your ability to lead—through good times and bad—**determines the legacy you leave behind.

Leadership is more than a title; it's the responsibility to create a clear vision, inspire unwavering commitment, and adapt with resilience when the storms come. The mindset you bring—your ability to remain focused, optimistic, and relentless in the face of adversity—shapes your success and those around you. And it's the culture you cultivate, one of loyalty, accountability, and shared purpose, that turns a collection of individuals into a powerful, unified team.

The Mindset That Shapes Your Future

A leader who refuses to accept mediocrity or fear failure is at the heart of every great empire. Your mindset is the bedrock of everything you build. It's your ability to envision the future before anyone else, see opportunities where others see obstacles, and commit to action regardless of the uncertainty ahead.

- **Relentless Focus**: Train your mind like a muscle. Eliminate distractions, sharpen your focus, and commit fully to your desired outcomes. Success begins with a single, unshakable decision to push forward.
- **Turning Setbacks into Lessons**: Adversity will come; when it does, true leaders step up. They don't shrink; they learn. Every setback contains a lesson that makes you better, sharper, and more prepared for the next challenge.
- **Long-Term Vision**: Building generational wealth requires patience. Avoid the temptation of short-term wins at the expense of long-term stability. Great

leaders play the long game and measure success in decades, not months.

The power of your mind—what you choose to believe, focus on, and act upon—determines whether you'll stumble or rise, build fleeting success or a lasting **Hard Asset Empire™**.

The Team That Becomes Your Ecosystem

No great empire is built alone. The success of your investments, deals, and strategies depends on the people you choose to surround yourself with. Brokers, attorneys, accountants, lenders, architects, and property managers are not just professionals but ecosystem partners. They amplify your strengths, fill your blind spots, and bring your vision to life.

The right team isn't just a group of skilled individuals; it's a loyal ecosystem that shares your values, trusts your leadership, and commits to mutual success.

- **Select Partners Who Align with Your Vision**: Skill and experience are critical, but alignment of values is non-negotiable. The best partnerships are built on shared goals, trust, and open communication.
- **Foster Loyalty**: Loyalty doesn't happen by accident—it's earned. Treat your team like partners,

reward their contributions, and stand by them through challenges. Loyalty creates strength, and strength creates enduring success.

- **Create a Winning Culture**: Leadership sets the tone for your team. Lead with clarity, recognize individual strengths, and build a culture where collaboration and excellence are the standard.

Leadership in Hard Times: The True Test

It's easy to lead when deals flow, cash is abundant, and success feels inevitable. But it's in the hard times—when markets tighten, deals fall through, and uncertainty clouds the future—that leadership matters most. Your team looks to you for stability, direction, and confidence.

Great leaders:

- **Communicate Transparently**: In tough times, silence creates fear. Be honest with your team, share the realities of the situation, and focus their energy on solutions.
- **Act Decisively**: Challenges demand action. Indecision is the greatest risk of all. Evaluate the situation, make a plan, and execute with confidence.
- **Stay Resilient and Optimistic**: Your mindset shapes the energy of your entire team. A calm, confident

leader inspires others to push forward, knowing that obstacles are temporary and success lies ahead.

The Legacy of Leadership

Leadership is not just about building wealth or closing deals. It's about leaving a lasting impact on your family, partners, community, and the next generation. Combining a powerful mindset, a loyal team, and the ability to lead through adversity creates a blueprint for success that extends far beyond yourself.

True wealth is not just financial. It's found in your partners' trust, your team's respect, and the knowledge that you've built something enduring. It's in the freedom to live life on your terms and the ability to provide for generations to come.

Final Reflections

As you close this book, know this: the tools and strategies shared here are your blueprint, but the construction is yours to navigate. Cultivate an indomitable will. Sharpen your mindset daily. Invest in relationships that matter. Lead with purpose, resilience, and vision. Let's continue that journey to customize your blueprint on my **Hard Asset Empire Blueprint™** courseware at www.alliancecgc.com/academy

now and use **COUPON CODE: "GIFTFROMBEN"** to get it for free!

Building your **Hard Asset Empire™** will not be easy, but it will be worth it. The opportunities are out there for those who are prepared, focused, and committed to action. Surround yourself with great people, lead them well, and embrace the challenges ahead.

The storms will come, but the empires built by strong minds, loyal teams, and unrelenting leaders will survive and thrive.

In the end, leadership is your ultimate weapon. It's how you turn visions into reality, challenges into victories, and wealth into legacy. Thank you for reading my book. Now go forward boldly, and remember: **Where there's a will, there's a way!**

~Ben Reinberg, CEO of Alliance Consolidated Group of Companies

Endnotes

1. John C. Maxwell, *The 21 Irrefutable Laws of Leadership* (HarperCollins Leadership, 1998), 75–80.
2. Marcus & Millichap, *2024 Commercial Real Estate Trends Report*, https://www.marcusmillichap.com/.
3. Andrew Baum, *Commercial Real Estate Investment: A Strategic Approach* (Routledge, 2009), 112–115.
4. Harvard Business Review, "Leadership Through Adversity," https://hbr.org/.
5. Urban Land Institute, *Emerging Trends in Real Estate 2024* (ULI, 2024), 80–85.

Appendices

BONUS CHAPTER:

The Due Diligence Cheatsheet

The most seasoned investors will tell you that success in real estate is not found in the deal's closing, but in the groundwork laid long before. Due diligence—the systematic verification, investigation, and risk assessment of a deal—is the most critical element of a sound investment strategy. It uncovers hidden pitfalls, ensures alignment with your financial goals, and ultimately protects your capital.

For sophisticated investors, due diligence goes beyond the basics. It is a rigorous, multi-layered process that blends financial analysis, property inspections, market intelligence, and legal review into a cohesive strategy. Whether you're acquiring multifamily real estate, issuing hard money loans, or funding complex value-add opportunities, due diligence mitigates risks and illuminates opportunities for maximizing returns.

This chapter will guide you through an advanced, step-by-step approach to due diligence. From analyzing financials and market trends to ensuring legal compliance and physical property health, this deep dive will arm you with the tools, checklists, and frameworks needed to execute flawlessly.

The Purpose and Importance of Due Diligence

At its core, due diligence confirms one critical fact: that the deal works. It answers questions such as:

- Does the property generate sufficient cash flow to meet your return expectations?
- Are there any physical, legal, or financial risks that could derail the investment?
- Is the market trending in favor of long-term growth and stability?

Failure to perform thorough due diligence can turn even the most promising deal into a financial disaster. Common pitfalls like overestimated income, underestimated expenses, title defects, or environmental hazards can wipe out potential profits and erode your capital base.

Due diligence empowers investors to make informed decisions based on verified data—not speculation. It minimizes uncertainty, boosts confidence, and increases the likelihood of achieving desired financial outcomes.

The Four Pillars of Due Diligence

A comprehensive due diligence process can be broken down into four main pillars: financial analysis, property condition, legal and title review, and market analysis. Below, we expand on each pillar with advanced recommendations and tools.

1. Financial Analysis

Financial due diligence determines whether the deal's numbers support your target returns. This involves verifying income, expenses, and future projections while stress-testing the property's ability to perform under various scenarios.

Key Steps to Financial Due Diligence:

- Verify Rent Rolls:

    - Cross-check leases with actual rent payments to identify discrepancies.

- Analyze lease expiration schedules to identify near-term vacancies.
- Look for incentives like rent abatements or concessions that may skew income figures.
- Review Income Statements and Tax Returns:

  - Request 2-3 years of historical income and expense statements.
  - Analyze trends in NOI growth, tenant churn, and expense patterns.
  - Compare seller-provided numbers against tax returns for verification.
- Inspect Operating Expenses:

  - Benchmark property expenses (e.g., taxes, utilities, insurance) against market norms.
  - Identify areas for cost reduction, such as renegotiating service contracts.
  - Analyze future CapEx requirements and budget contingencies.
- Stress-Test Cash Flow Scenarios:

  - Model worst-case outcomes include rent declines, rising vacancies, or higher interest rates.

- Ensure the property generates sufficient income to cover debt service and operating costs.

Tools for Financial Due Diligence:

- **Stessa:** Automates property income and expense tracking.
- **Appfolio Investment Management:** Provides detailed property performance reports.
- **CoStar Analytics:** Benchmark operating expenses and market rents against comparable properties.

2. Physical Condition

The physical condition of a property can make or break an investment. Overlooking critical repairs or environmental hazards can lead to unexpected capital expenditures that drain your cash flow.

Key Steps for Physical Inspections:

- Hire Professional Inspectors:

    - Conduct a comprehensive inspection of roofing, HVAC, plumbing, electrical, and structural integrity.
    - Use specialists for specific concerns (e.g., foundation engineers or mold assessors).

- Perform Environmental Assessments:

  - Order a Phase I Environmental Site Assessment (ESA) to uncover contamination risks.
  - Conduct Phase II testing if initial findings indicate hazards like asbestos, mold, or soil issues.
- Evaluate Deferred Maintenance:

  - Create a line-item list of required repairs and renovation costs.
  - Prioritize high-impact upgrades that improve property value and tenant satisfaction.
- CapEx Projections:

  - Plan for long-term capital improvements (e.g., HVAC replacement, roof repairs).
  - Allocate 5–10% of annual revenue toward CapEx reserves.

Tools for Physical Due Diligence:

- **BlueTape**: Automates CapEx planning and project tracking.
- **Buildium:** Tracks property maintenance schedules and vendor relationships.

---

3. Legal and Title Review

Legal issues can derail an otherwise perfect deal. Clean title, zoning compliance, and lease review are critical to the legal due diligence process.

Key Steps for Legal Due Diligence:

- Order a Title Search:

  - Identify liens, encumbrances, easements, or unresolved claims against the property.
  - Use title insurance to mitigate risks.
- Confirm Zoning Compliance:

  - Verify current zoning permits intended use (e.g., multifamily, retail).

- Review upcoming zoning changes or development plans that could impact the property.
- Lease Review:

  - Confirm tenant compliance with lease obligations.
  - Identify unfavorable lease clauses, such as early termination or caps on rent escalations.
- Regulatory Compliance:

  - Verify permits, inspections, and code compliance for renovations or additions.

Tools for Legal Due Diligence:

- **Prophia**: Streamlines lease abstraction and analytics.
- **TitlePro247**: Provides instant access to title reports.

---

4. Market Analysis

Even the best property fails if the market fundamentals are weak. Understanding supply, demand, economic trends, and tenant dynamics is critical to predicting long-term performance.

Key Steps for Market Due Diligence:

- Study Demographic Data:

    - Analyze population growth, job creation, and household income trends.
    - Use tools like U.S. Census Bureau and Esri for detailed demographic insights.
- Examine Market Trends:

    - Study vacancy rates, absorption rates, and rental growth trends.
    - Evaluate economic drivers like major employers, infrastructure, and redevelopment projects.
- Identify Supply and Demand Imbalances:

    - Assess pipeline development projects that may increase competition.
    - Compare property performance to similar assets in the area.
- Forecast Long-Term Growth:

    - Identify markets with favorable long-term trends, such as population booms or employment surges.

Tools for Market Due Diligence:

- CBRE Market Reports: Comprehensive market data and projections.
- CoStar and Reonomy: Detailed market analysis tools for vacancy and rent data.

Avoiding Common Due Diligence Pitfalls

1. Skipping Inspections: *Always inspect. Seller assurances are not enough.*
2. Ignoring Market Trends: *Never assume rents or values will rise—verify with data.*
3. Underestimating CapEx: *Budget for repairs, renovations, and long-term improvements.*
4. Failing to Stress-Test: *Model worst-case cash flow scenarios to test property performance.*
5. Neglecting Legal Review: *Hire professionals to vet title reports, leases, and zoning compliance.*

The Power of Due Diligence: Lessons Learned

A war story from my career underlines the value of thorough due diligence. A $15 million multifamily deal appeared perfect on paper: solid rent rolls, strong location, and seemingly minimal deferred maintenance. However, during the physical inspection, our team uncovered systemic plumbing issues requiring $2 million in repairs—unforeseen by the seller's disclosures. Because we performed rigorous due diligence, we negotiated a price reduction that protected our capital and allowed for planned repairs without compromising cash flow.

The lesson? Always dig deeper. Due diligence transforms risk into opportunity.

Due diligence is the ultimate tool for protecting and growing your **Hard Asset Empire™**. It is a rigorous, multi-faceted process that transforms uncertainty into informed decision-making. From verifying financials and inspecting property health to analyzing market trends and securing legal safeguards, no detail is too small to investigate.

For hard money lenders and real estate investors alike, due diligence eliminates the guesswork, mitigates risk, and positions you to seize opportunities confidently. *The most successful investors approach due diligence as non-negotiable*—because in *Hard Asset Empire™ building*, success is earned through rigorous preparation and attention to detail.

Endnotes

1. Robert Irwin, *Tips and Traps When Buying Real Estate* (McGraw-Hill, 2006), 145–150.
2. Andrew Baum, *Commercial Real Estate Investment: A Strategic Approach* (Routledge, 2009), 85–90.
3. Urban Land Institute, *Due Diligence Best Practices in Real Estate Transactions* (ULI, 2021), 35–40.
4. Marcus & Millichap, *2024 Real Estate Market Trends Report*, https://www.marcusmillichap.com/.
5. Deloitte, "Navigating Legal Risks in Real Estate Transactions," https://www2.deloitte.com/.
6. CBRE, *Real Estate Outlook 2024*, https://www.cbre.com/.
7. Esri, *Demographic Trends and Economic Growth*, https://www.esri.com/.
8. Federal Title, "The Importance of Title Reports in CRE Deals," Federal Title Blog, January 2024.
9. CoStar Group, "Market Insights and Data Analysis," https://www.costar.com/.

Glossary of Key Terms

Real Estate, Lease, and Finance Terms

- **Triple Net Lease (NNN)** – Tenant pays base rent plus property taxes, insurance, and maintenance.
- **Gross Lease (Full-Service Lease)** – Landlord covers all operating expenses, and tenant pays a fixed rent.
- **Modified Gross Lease** – A mix of NNN and Gross Lease where tenants and landlords share operating expenses.
- **Common Area Maintenance (CAM) Fees** – Tenant's share of costs for maintaining shared spaces like lobbies and parking lots.
- **Usable Square Footage (USF)** – The actual space a tenant occupies.
- **Rentable Square Footage (RSF)** – The USF plus some common spaces.
- **Load Factor** – The percentage of common areas added to USF to calculate RSF.

Investment & Financial Terms

- **Cap Rate (Capitalization Rate)** – A property's annual net operating income (NOI) divided by its purchase price, used to evaluate investment returns.
- **Net Operating Income (NOI)** – Gross rental income minus operating expenses (excluding mortgage payments).

- **Cash-on-Cash Return** – Annual cash flow divided by the initial investment, useful for measuring returns on leveraged investments.
- **Internal Rate of Return (IRR)** – The rate at which an investment breaks even in present value terms.
- **Debt Service Coverage Ratio (DSCR)** – NOI divided by total debt service; used by lenders to assess risk.
- **Loan-to-Value Ratio (LTV)** – The mortgage amount divided by property value indicates loan risk.
- **Capital Expenditures (CapEx)** – Funds used for major property improvements or replacements.

Property Types & Development Terms

- **Class A, B, C Buildings** – A classification system based on quality, location, and amenities:
- **Class A** – High-end, well-located, and modern.
- **Class B** – Good quality but slightly older.
- **Class C** – Older properties needing renovation.
- **Build-to-Suit** – A custom-developed property to meet a specific tenant's needs.
- **Core, Core-Plus, Value-Add, Opportunistic Investments** – A risk classification for CRE investments:
- **Core** – Low-risk, stable income properties.
- **Core-Plus** – Slightly higher risk, minor value-add potential.
- **Value-Add** – Moderate risk with renovation opportunities.
- **Opportunistic** – High-risk, high-reward projects (e.g., ground-up developments).

Legal & Regulatory Terms

- **Easements** – Legal rights for a third party to use a property (e.g., utility companies).
- **Zoning Laws** – Regulations governing property use (e.g., commercial, industrial, residential).
- **Entitlements** – Government approvals for development projects.
- **Right of First Refusal (ROFR)** – A tenant's or investor's option to match any third-party purchase offer.

Market & Transaction Terms

- **Absorption Rate** – The rate at which available space is leased over a specific time.
- **Tenant Improvement (TI) Allowance** – Funds the landlord provides for leasehold improvements.
- **Anchor Tenant** – A major tenant (e.g., a big retailer) that drives traffic to a commercial property.
- **Sale-Leaseback** – A strategy where an owner sells a property and leases it back to maintain operational control while freeing up capital.

Crypto Slang

- **Diamond Hands:** A term used to describe investors who hold onto an asset despite volatility or market downturns, believing in its long-term value.

- **HODL**: A crypto term meaning "Hold On for Dear Life," encouraging investors not to sell during market fluctuations.
- **Sats (Satoshis)**: The smallest unit of Bitcoin, equal to 0.00000001 BTC. Named after Bitcoin's pseudonymous creator, Satoshi Nakamoto.
- **Pump-and-Dump**: A manipulative scheme where the price of an asset is artificially inflated (pumped) and then sold off (dumped), leaving late buyers at a loss.
- **Mooning** is a slang term describing an asset's significant upward price movement. "When Bitcoin moons, we all win."

Urban Dictionary-Style Terms

- **Skin in the Game**: Personal financial investment in a project, ensuring alignment of interests between stakeholders.
- **Going Hard**: The point at which an earnest-money deposit becomes non-refundable.
- **YOLO Trade**: High-risk investment decisions based on the idea that "You Only Live Once." Often discouraged in real estate and hard money investing.
- FOMO (Fear of Missing Out): A psychological driver causing investors to chase trends or assets due to fear of being left out.
- Shark Repellent: Protective measures taken in a deal to prevent predatory practices by competitors or bad actors.

Additional Resources

Websites and Newsletters

- **Alliance Intelligence Newsletter:** www.subscribetoben.com - Industry insights and premium reports and content from Ben Reinberg and the Alliance Intelligence team.
- **Alliance Academy:** www.alliancecgc.com/academy - e-courses (freemium subscription), live summits and webinars, and 24/7 deal mentorship using the Ben Reinberg digital twin and Alliance resource library of term sheets, diligence checklists, and proven strategies.
- **Marcus & Millichap**: www.marcusmillichap.com – Industry insights and market trends in commercial real estate.
- **BiggerPockets**:www.biggerpockets.com – Community forums, tools, and resources for real estate investors.
- **FRED (Federal Reserve Economic Data):** fred.stlouisfed.org – Economic data and trends useful for market analysis.
- **Deloitte Insights**: www2.deloitte.com – In-depth research on real estate and finance trends.
- **Wealth Matters 3.0** www.wealthmatterstome.com

Courses and Certifications

- **Alliance Academy:** www.alliancecgc.com/academy - e-courses (freemium subscription), live summits and webinars, and 24/7 deal mentorship using the Ben Reinberg digital twin and Alliance resource library of term sheets, diligence checklists, and proven strategies.
- **CCIM Institute**: Certified Commercial Investment Member designation for advanced investment analysis and market expertise.
- **Urban Land Institute (ULI)**: Educational programs focusing on real estate trends and development strategies.
- **Coursera and edX**: Online platforms offering courses in real estate finance, data analytics, and blockchain technology.

THE END